HACKNEY CHILD

'*Hackney Child* is a shocking reminder of what some children are subjected to as they grow up. The scars can last a lifetime and there is no certainty they will ever heal. The best way is always to fight back. Hope Daniels has done this and displayed great courage in reliving the events of her childhood through this book. I wish her all the success in the world.'

Harry Keeble, bestselling author of *Baby X*

'*Hackney Child* tells us the story of Hope as she grew up in the care system. It is a terrible indictment of our society that children should suffer such cruelty, especially when being "cared for" by people who should protect them. I pray, that by telling her story, Hope can find some peace because I believe this story needed to be told. Have a happy life, Miss Daniels.'

Cassie Harte, *Sunday Times* number one bestselling author

'An insightful look into one girl's journey into the care system in the eighties, Hope's story shows the maturity and opportunistic attitude some vulnerable children undertake in order to thrive, the powerful impact that small decisions can have on a child's life and the on-going struggles care children face even as adults. As her name exemplifies, Hope's compelling account fortifies that every marginalized child has a chance to overcome adversity.'

Ruth Stivey, The Who Cares? Trust

HACKNEY CHILD

A TRUE TALE OF SURVIVING POVERTY AND THE CARE SYSTEM

Hope Daniels and Morag Livingstone

SIMON &
SCHUSTER

London · New York · Sydney · Toronto · New Delhi

A CBS COMPANY

This edition published in Great Britain by Simon & Schuster UK Ltd, 2014
A CBS COMPANY

Originally self-published by Livingstone Media, 2012

1 3 5 7 9 10 8 6 4 2

Simon & Schuster UK Ltd
1st Floor
222 Gray's Inn Road
London WC1X 8HB

www.simonandschuster.co.uk

Simon & Schuster Australia

Sydney

Simon & Schuster India
New Delhi

A CIP catalogue record for this book is available from the British Library.
ISBN (Paperback): 978-1-47112-983-4
ISBN (Ebook): 978-1-47112-987-2

Typeset by Hewer Text UK Ltd, Edinburgh
Printed in the UK by CPI (UK) Ltd, Croydon CR0 4YY

While this book gives a faithful account of the author's experiences,
some names and details have been changed to protect the privacy
of the individuals involved.

Hope dedicates this book to:

her granddaughter
and has told this story for all the children
in the care system

Morag dedicates this book to:

Hope

CONTENTS

PREFACE

I was born and bred in Hackney. I was not from the posh part of Hackney – I grew up in the seventies as a child on an estate with other families from different races and cultural backgrounds. For me, childhood was something to be enjoyed, and no matter what the struggles were that parents went through, there were some fundamentals for bringing up children – parents provided a home, regular food, warmth and love; and taught us to show some respect to ourselves and others.

Hackney has a rich, diverse melting pot of people from different races, cultures and classes. It is vibrant and alive, yet I have a kind of love–hate relationship with it today because, woven within its colourful fabric, Hackney, like other areas of London and beyond, has its fair share of problems: child abuse, drugs, alcoholism, gun crime, mental health issues, prostitution . . . It seems almost unbelievable that as a child I knew little of the ingrained poverty that surrounded me and impacted on the lives of children on a daily basis. Perhaps I was simply naive. Or maybe I was protected from the harsh realities of life.

I met Hope (not her real name) when I became her social worker. During our introductions, before our meeting, she insisted on my sending her a photo of myself, which I did. I met a sixteen-year-old Hope, who asked endless questions; seemed very focused on her future; and was bright, sharp, humorous, inquisitive and, last but not least, determined. I adored her spirit. Underneath this exterior I sensed her vulnerabilities, and I learnt more about her need to have constant, caring adult figures in her life. Although in this day and age it wouldn't be recommended, I have remained a constant figure in Hope's life – a kind of social aunt.

Hackney Child is Hope Daniels' first book about the early part of her life. It demonstrates her highly developed survival skills, which can teach us a great deal about resilience and resourcefulness. Although much has changed since the seventies and eighties, this book is an account of a life that, as I write, sadly continues to resonate with the experiences of some children and young people in the care system.

If we want to improve our understanding of the conflicts between the inner and outer world of the children and young people we work with, the true voice of the child must be heard. Here is a book that offers us that opportunity: it is a must-read for all social care and health professionals.

By Hope's social worker, 'S'

Few will have the greatness to bend history itself, but each of us can work to change a small portion of events, and in the total of all those acts will be written the history of this generation.

Robert F. Kennedy

LETTER TO LILY

Dear Lily,

This morning I watched you being born, my dear new grand-daughter.

I feel the miracle of life as the next generation arrives, and I am overwhelmed with joy and, strangely, a compunction to write. I have a forceful need to speak to you through the pages of this book (although I still think of it more as a diary than a book). These are not words that I am capable of speaking, but I do need to release them. These are not words for now, but for when you are older, but I do feel the need to write them now. From the moment I knew I was pregnant with your mother, I loved her with all my heart, and I still do. You are part of a beautiful new generation. Your mother grew up in a loving, caring home, and this is where the past stops.

When I was eighteen, I had access to information about my life that I couldn't deal with. I left the room having read three files of information I could not cope with at that age. At twenty-two I *accessed the files again. It has taken me until now, as a grand-mother at thirty-five years old, a mother of two in a happy, steady relationship, to reconcile the information contained in those files and live with who my family is, was. Your Nana has deliberately avoided her past, but now you are here everything is different. When you are older, I want you to know from where you have come. I want you to know I tried to reach out to others like me. I tried to look after children, wards of court, kids in care. After all, they are all just children.*

I have lived thus far with so many stereotypes. By the nature of my birth, I have been labelled, branded, expected to falter, fail, and underachieve. Statistics for children in care are never positive.

When your parent is the State, such statistics hold you back. They give you a name, a reputation. Everyone presumes you will carry on the generational cycle of 'following your mother'. These stats are actually the real lives of kids damaged before they go into care, not damaged because of being in care. I proved them wrong because I broke that cycle. That's no mean achievement considering everything. Yet my ambitions were always high for someone in my position. As a child, my dreams of the future consisted of achieving a 'normal' family life. I did not under-stand what that meant at the time, but you will, as your mummy does, and for this, it's all been worth it. My hopes did not extend beyond achieving a safe normality, and having choices. I'm happy this has been achieved. It is strange to think that all we, as a family, have, is something taken for granted by so many, yet also something that my parents were incapable, by virtue of their history, of providing.

Without being given a choice, a person surviving on the fringes of society in Hackney grows up quickly. Mature beyond their years, yet, even now, in so many ways, in adulthood still a vulnerable child. I can spot a child who has been in care from 40 yards away. I want you to be a child's child and have the joy of love and being loved. Most importantly, your parents and your grandparents can provide you with a normal family life. We have worked hard to achieve this for you. It is a life that past generations could only dream of.

We carried the burden of the labels given to us, as you will carry clean clothes on your back. We met the expectations of these stereotypes with all the flair and panache of the Barbie doll I dreamt of owning when I was a girl. Tomorrow I will buy you a pink doll, and a set of new clothes.

Unable to cope with my parents' chaotic life, care was the better option. Yet I have, since I left care, hidden my past. I refused to disclose anything about being in care.

That stigma, that shame I felt, has permeated every action and decision in my life. As I write this, nearly twenty years after leaving care, I realize I've not always told the truth about my life. I've created countless fantasies, sometimes because I just didn't know what the truth was. This book – these collections of memories, letters to you and extracts from my files – will allow me to be honest with my children and you, the first of my grandchildren. Perhaps for the first time, I will be able to be honest with myself. Only by facing the past can I move freely into the future, with you, my gentle flower.

A happy memory was created today, joining other memories, necessary but often painful. Memories, often triggered by a noise, a sound, the bus number, music – whatever the trigger, what follows is painful. Yet I cannot seem to avoid them.

Certain people have a fascination with my earliest memories. Memories are enquired after, as old friends should be, by well-meaning, inquisitive people. It is as if the earliest memory *reveals the person of today, providing some indication of the map of the life that follows. I want your earliest memory to be joyful. I want every, or at least the majority, of your memories to be happy. I want your family home to be a true family. Whatever else happens, I want you to feel your family loves you. This, my precious grandchild, is the promise, the gift, I am able to give to you.*

Your Nana, Hope

1

MEMORY

Report for young person coming to notice of police, 18 August 1983

At about 11.30 a.m. three children walked into the Stoke Newington police station. The children are known to the police as children of [BLANK], a prostitute, and [BLANK], a convicted thief.

The young girl, Hope, nine years old, demanded to see her social worker and be taken into care as she and her two brothers (five) and (seven) could no longer live at home.

A Place of Safety Order was placed on them and Hope and her brothers have been given into the care of social workers and transferred to Chesterfields Children's Home, Highgate.

Social services files. Memory, 1993

Ever since 1983, when I walked into a police station, at nine years old, and demanded that my brothers and I be put into care, I've been obsessed with reading my social work files.

Here they are. My life stacked up in front of me. On a table, unstable piles of brown and green files, each pile a foot high. Files, full to the brim. Four piles of three and one on the side equal thirteen. The windowless room is no more than 6 feet by 6 feet. Pale, pleasant yellow-painted walls that hold no comfort for me. Apart from the clock on the wall, a desk, a chair and the memories in my files, I have no company. A smile crosses my lips as the faint smell of polish reaches my nostrils. Nice how they cleaned the room up a bit to try to hide the smell of musk that permeates every social worker's interview room.

Closing the heavy, blue-grey, wooden door behind me blocks out the disruptive noise of people with chaotic lives, heading towards an interview with their designated social worker. At the end of that interview, there will be white paper added to their file, white paper that maybe results from the yellow paper, already filed, received from the police when they wrote their report.

Nope, the files look no different even if I tilt my head sideways. There are more white pieces of paper than yellow: that's something.

On the surface they are still just old files from before and after my birth, from the seventies and eighties, which makes sense, as they are about me, about my family, before and after I was born.

We've been known to social services for a long time. Pieces of paper other people have written on, social workers, lawyers, judges, therapists, psychologists, carefully bound and stored. My life, my parents' lives, my siblings' lives. White and yellow paper, dog-eared at the corners, evidence that someone has taken an interest.

Who? Why?

I laugh out loud at the absurdity. All the time we were with my parents we were told to keep quiet, not to tell anyone about life at home. But by the sheer fact there are so many files, each no less than three inches thick, means that there is, was, no secret to keep after all. The fantasies about a loving family that I created to tell other people, so that I could cope myself, were they all for nothing? The reasons for a continued life in care, the happenings of my life in care, my parents' lives, and the reasons they could not cope, haven't been a secret for other people. It's just been kept secret from me.

I've had no formal input to these files and yet here they are, waiting. They've been waiting here throughout all the time I've been obsessing about them, all my time in, and after, I was in care. I'm no different in this regard from many children in the care system, all obsessed with obtaining and reading their files.

These brown and green folders protecting their precious cargo, sitting on a speckled grey Formica-topped desk supported by four thin grey metal legs.

I wait for my old friend, inner strength, to come so I can pick up my courage and open these files. As I wait for the familiar voice to enter my head to say, 'Just get on with it!' I imagine the social worker, my lovely supportive social worker, Bella, receiving confirmation to release these files, to provide me, Hope – eighteen years old, born in Hackney to alcoholic parents – with access to the files about my childhood.

She is moving them two by two from a locked cabinet, to a room with which I'm not familiar, but it is the best she can find considering the demands placed upon the Hackney social work department. I see her deciding where to place them, arranging them landscape across the desk, no, portrait, so the small end faces the door. I feel her worry about the positioning, as if this decision will lessen the impact of what is inside, documented, known by others but not by me. She places the files in date order, with care, with respect. She waits for me to arrive, by appointment.

I've dreamt of this moment, fought for this time to come. Now it's here and the files are no more than four feet away from me, I do as I always do in a difficult situation: I work myself up into a panic. I can't. I back away from the files; my hand is turning the handle of the door to go. Something changes inside me.

This is stupid. I've waited years for this.

So many unanswered questions. The answers are there. Looking over my shoulder towards the files, it's as if my past is beckoning me, persuading me finally to squash the obsession. I breathe out until I am calm. My vision blurs, a single tear escapes.

I can't do this. I can't. Come, on girl, you must. I can.

The second hand on the clock ticks. The big hand has moved fifteen minutes, and I haven't moved at all. Staring, just staring. A complex set of emotions that I'm unable to process engulfs me. I'm trying to cope, to be brave, when all I want is someone to comfort me, to take control. Instead I stand, waiting for the sign, a physical reaction that occurs after I've been flattened by an experience. Following fear, a momentary silence, then my body fills with warm calm and I just get on with doing what needs to be done. I am standing, I am staring. I count the files again, delaying the inevitable.

Decisions made for me by social workers, foster parents, judges, are between these pages. I want, have always wanted, to know what they really thought, think. How did they record decisions I made out of fear, low self-esteem or just to buck the system, about when I ran away and the other times I rebelled, led others into a course of action. Is this all documented?

Did they note that I almost became a lawyer? How did they write about me? Were they kind? Were they professional? What did they think of my mum? My dad?

Did they see past the laughter and the overconfident, capable youth to the scared child inside, who just wanted to be noticed, to be loved?

My feet feel heavy. I can hear my mother entering my head. Expertly I push her away before she can overwhelm me. An image of my pregnancy scan, my perfect child to come, replaces her. The feelings I associate with my mother's presence dissolve. I remember why I'm doing this.

I am now building a family of my own, and more than ever I want to know the truth of who I, who we, are. I think over what I've achieved – a normal family life. My unborn child is already loved, will be cherished and have a good, clean and safe home. I'm proud of that. I know if I hadn't gone into care, history would have been repeated from one generation to the next. I want to reclaim my life from these files. To take control of the reality – as reality is set out in these files – however bad. I want to know now. I step towards these files just as I walked into a police station at nine years old and demanded to see my social worker. My hand reaches forward: I place it on top of the first pile. I'm back in the police station, nine years old, grubby hand reaching up to the counter.

Reassurance.

The outside of the folder feels like reassurance. The police counter is reassuring. A wave of security enfolds me. The policeman tells me, I don't have to go home. Confident now, I sit, dump my bag on the floor and pull a file from the top of the pile. Right to left, the folder opens. Right to left the policeman opens his folder. I'm here looking at the first page of my officially documented history. The yellow police report is there. I'm nine. The policeman is writing. I'm eighteen and I'm reading, for the first time, what he has written.

I take notes but, after the third file, I give up. Tears streaming down my face. Unable to cope with the emotions triggered by my discovery. I am unable to read any more through my tears, and I know I have read enough. I don't recognize this family in these files. Yet I know them intimately. I know it's us, but there appears so much I didn't know about my parents.

What is the truth?

I am eighteen, I'm here and, despite my baby being due in a matter of weeks, I feel terribly alone.

I sit. I sit, frozen.

My hand moves first to my mouth and, as I have so often done, I wipe away my tears with both palms, eyes to chin, and hope when I leave this room no one will notice my tears have been spent.

I pick up my bag, not knowing if I will ever look at these files again. Not caring. For now I know enough. It seems I knew then, at nine, what I know now – for all the faults and challenges of the care system – sometimes going into care gives better chances, is just better, than living at home.

A party, 1977

It's dark. I'm feeling secure and warm under a blanket of coats from the partygoers. The music is happy, not the sad Elvis Presley or even sadder Tom Jones that we get at home. Like home, the children are upstairs; unlike home, we play with the reassurance of hearing adult voices drift upstairs alongside a winter warmth that fills this house.

Laughter.

It's been a good evening spent playing with other kids: maybe Mum will let us play with them again. Tired, my younger brother Jack and I lie down under the pile of coats, each belonging to a guest. The material soft. Beautiful smells of perfume caress the clothes and my nose. I drift off. Jack beside me.

I wake up. The music has stopped. Both hands on the square white clock on the table are pointing to the ceiling. There is an argument going on downstairs. I can't hear my parents.

Please don't be fighting. I want to play with the children again.

My mum is always fighting. I strain to hear her. She's not there, I'm sure of it.

Whew. We'll get to come back here then. If Mum's not there fighting then . . . Mum? Where's Mum then? If she's not fighting, she can't be there.

Scrambling out of the bed, I see the pile of coats is not as high as when we crawled under it. I pull another layer of fine-smelling, soft coat over Jack's sleeping body. The carpet feels lovely on the soles of my feet. The room smells clean. I open the bedroom door and the smell of cigarette smoke, booze, a party, the smell similar to home, greets me.

I strain my head round the door. Can't hear. Move forward. Sit on the stairs.

'What do you mean . . . they bloody left them here?'

'That's what she said, Michael.'

'What the fuck does that mean, Maureen? Who does that? Leave their kids?'

'She said she didn't want them.'

'What the FUCK. What are we meant to do?'

'We've sent our John round to see them, and that's what she's said. She forgot to take them home, so we can have them. She's drunk, Michael.'

'So are fuckin' we, but we don't just leave our kids. We'd never leave them. Who the fuck . . . what the fuck?'

'Michael, calm down. The little ones are sleeping. We don't want to wake them now, do we? We can let them sleep tonight. When she's sober in the morning she will wonder where her kids are, she will come and get them, and we shall just say they had a sleepover.'

Tears, snot, streak down my face. I creep back under the coats. Hoping no one will find me. Hoping someone will care. Light, as the door opens, and no light as it closes. Someone is in the room. Maureen, I know her perfume. The last of the coats are lifted from us. A blanket replaces them. She touches my head, gently, motherly.

The door opens, the door closes. A tear escapes from my eyes at the kindness. Footsteps down the stairs.

'It will be all right, you'll see, Michael.'

For two days, people leave the house and come back with a shake of the head, and a resigned, 'No one there.' The initial excitement of staying somewhere else, with other children to play with, wears off as people stop speaking to us. Instead, there are whispers in the corner. Mutterings in the kitchen. We sit, we play. We sleep on the sofa. Warm. A biscuit and milk thrust, not often enough, our way. Two sleeps later, my elder, teenage brother, Phillip, comes to fetch us.

The excitement of seeing him, at being wanted after all, means we skip home, slowing at the end of our street. From this end to the other, where our house is, we can hear the music. Tom Jones, Elvis Presley, means one thing. My parents, drunk. With every step the feelings sink lower down through my legs. With every step, we all slow, delaying the opening of the front door as much as we can.

A summer's day, 1979
Out of my bedroom window I can see my neighbours playing in their garden. The sound of two children and splashing water help me feel the heat of summer as it starts to caress my skin through the window. Their joyful screams bounce over the fence and right through the glass. They catch me, and my attention, as I stand in the room I share with my parents, staring at the wardrobe that is my mother's and not for looking inside. Jesus is here too, looking as he always does down from his cross on the wall. He is the

only one that sees me every day resisting the temptation to find out what is on the other side of the wardrobe doors.

Their laughter pulls me to the window. I stand in the shadows of the curtains looking down at them, feeling my eyes widening at the colours in their garden. Flowers bloom: red, yellow, orange neatly arranged around three sides, by the garden fence. In one corner of the garden, it is different. This area is still green, but it looks like a field and there are a lot of green leaves sticking up from the ground, all covered in nets. Rhubarb, there is rhubarb there, too. In front of the earth holding the big plants and the rhubarb stretches bright green grass, cut short and even like Wimbledon tennis lawns – I saw it on the TV in the window of Radio Rentals.

The grass reaches all the way from the back of the garden to the house. In the middle of the clean-cut bright-green grass are two playing children, each with a mass of curly black hair and the most beautiful brown skin that seems to glow clean, and a paddling pool. Its sides are bright yellow, as bright as the crayon we have at school to draw the sun. It's full of water filled from a hose that lies abandoned but ready to work again when needed. I sigh. I rub the glass with my sleeve to see better. I watch a bird dancing around in water on a table. The table looks like it has been made just for the birds to play in and for no other reason. I am impressed. My head moves from side to side to get a better view. I avoid looking at the overgrown chaos in our garden – we have no birds. Not only are there birds in their garden, but the people who live there have even given a special place, right next to the kitchen window, where the birds can play.

The birds dart in and out of the water table. I follow the

line of flight backwards and see that they approach tentatively. First they sit on the fence, looking in every direction, checking they aren't going to be caught, then they dart to the edge of the water, sitting for a moment on the brim of the table. SPLASH! They have done it. They do their thing. I think the birds move just like Dad has taught us to move around the shops when getting our dinner without money. We look around to make sure we don't get caught and we also try to look normal while we grab a packet from the shelves. We, like the birds, can do this all at the same time. I laugh out loud. Maybe Dad taught the birds too. The children hear me and look up. I dart back so they don't see me watching. Too late. They shout up at me.

'Do you want to come over and play?'

A mixture of excitement and fear overtakes me. My mother will kill me if she finds out: we know we aren't allowed to talk to black people. She says they take our jobs and everything. She calls them niggers – I wince when she spits the word out. She didn't say I couldn't play with them though. They are our neighbours, so she couldn't mean them. The girl asked me, so I can tell Mum they talked to me first. But she won't find out: she's out getting drunk as usual.

Thoughts stream through my head: *I don't know. Mum does say we're not allowed to talk to them, but what about when they talk to us? It's a hot day. They have a paddling pool. They spoke to me first. They invited me. I will come back before night-time.*

I stand and look through the window at two eager smiling faces, hands beckoning, welcoming me to their perfect grass, paddling pool and play-water for birds. They stand staring up as I stare down. Three big smiles on both sides of the fence. Communicating through glass. From their mouths, a friendly, 'Come on!'

That does it. I pull the window as wide open as someone who has just turned five can, stretch my blonde hair through, pop my head slightly to the right and, with my best cheeky smile, the one the man in the post office tells me is all blue eyes and dimples, shout back: 'OK, yeah. I will. Give me a min.'

I throw the window down again before they change their minds and, still grinning but conscious of this act being my first rebellion, I feel a little bit sick. I rush to the bathroom, cool my face with water, feel a little less sick, and scrub my face with my hands. I strip ready for the pool and run out of the back door in my underpants.

Some beer crates provide a good ladder to get me to the top of the fence. I swing my legs over. First sitting on the fence, looking in every direction, checking my parents are not going to catch me and that I can jump far enough not to damage her flowers. I go for it.

Whew, I'm over the flowers.

We all dart, laughing, to the edge of the water. We three stand, each in our pants with elastic trim, grinning at each other for a moment next to the brim of the pool, checking with each other's eyes that it's OK to jump in. SPLASH. We've done it. With that first soaking in the summer sun, we make new friends. I feel lucky, 'cos I make two new friends; as they know each other already, they make only one new friend.

We run around the garden until we are dry, and go in

the water again. We three repeat this fun-filled ritual each time with an ever-increasing volume of laughter until the pool is empty of its contents and the grass is nicely watered. We jump out of the pool onto the water-laden grass and enjoy the cool splash of mud up our legs. While we fill the pool up again with water from the hose, we lie on a dry patch of grass on our backs looking at the electric-blue sky and making starfish with our legs and arms. Their mum creates a shadow so we open our eyes to find juice. She is dancing along to Lovers Rock music, British reggae. I've heard her say, 'I like it, sounds happy,' and she looks happy. She wants us to join in and we do. She asks if I want something to eat, and I must have been polite as spicy chicken and rice and peas, as she calls it, appear for us all. We are told to wash our hands. Their downstairs toilet smells of talcum powder; they have soap on the sink and loads of toilet paper, some of it even in a basket at the side. We only have squares of newspaper, ripped up, and left by the toilet.

Cor, this house is well posh. Which one do I use?

I remember not to act surprised and when I get my plate of food, I say 'Thank you' like the other children say at school.

I look at my plate and feel sure my portion is bigger than the others. I smile at the lady and say 'Thank you' again. She smiles back and says, 'You are very welcome.' I am beaming and very pleased with my new friends and their mother. They must be very rich to have brown bread and to eat in the afternoon. We three sit on the grass, cross-legged, and eat our food as Radio 1 plays through the open window. Their mother is dancing to all the songs. I am happy they spoke to me first, so now I can speak to them and play and eat.

I say it's nice that it has been sunny since my birthday. This allows me to tell them about my birthday being on the 20th of July, two sleeps ago. I was five. They tell me their birthdays are in winter. They are twins and they are four. They don't go to school yet. They ask again about my birthday. I say we had a nice day because Mum and Dad stayed at home. No one asks me about a party, which I'm glad about, and I don't tell them I didn't have one, though after I went to bed I could hear through the floorboards that Mum and Dad had a party for me. I tell them I got a doll. I don't tell them she had no arms and that Dad got it from the skip. I tell them we had a nice tea of corned-beef hash and radishes, which is Dad's favourite thing to cook. They screw up their noses at that, so I change the subject and as we have all finished eating I say, 'Beat you to the pool!' and we all run at the same time as I lick what they call jerk chicken, Grandma's recipe, from my face into my mouth. I marvel that their grandma has a recipe and that their mother cooks. My grandma does not have a recipe, but she has a tin for sweets, and I have never seen my mother cook, so I don't say a thing.

I also didn't tell them that on my birthday I heard Dad say to Mum that he didn't have any trouble getting the stuff. I knew at the time this was good news, as when he or Mum has any trouble – as nice as the coppers are to me – the cops come to see my parents and most times take one of them away, so I wouldn't want the cops visiting on my birthday.

But I didn't tell my new friends this, though even now

I don't know why I knew not to tell them. I just knew not to tell.

Like the grass, it is a perfect afternoon. So perfect I forget the time. As the sun turns from white-hot to red yellow, insects rise to bite and the lovely warm day moves into evening, with the smell of a storm being carried in on the breeze. Along with the change in temperature, my mother arrives home.

From where my new friends stood earlier in the day to call me over to their house, I look up and there she is. She is standing where I had stood, at the window looking down. She is taller than me, because I am just five and she is my mother. She can open the window faster than me and her face is not smiling. The red lipstick screams at me so everyone can hear:

'Why are you over there with those black fucking cunts?'

I flinch, knowing this is wrong, this language, and her treatment of people. She sees me flinch.

Mum looks mad. I am in big trouble.

My head falls in shame, my chin on my chest. The crown of my head leads me on my way home. I mumble an apology. But the family have regrouped and are already fading away. From the corner of my eye I see their mother ushering her chicks back into the safety of their powder puff home. Her dark eyes are a mixture of pity, hate and fear. The birds are long gone. The happiness of the garden swept away by what I will soon learn to be my mother's screaming racism.

By the time I get to the fence and try to climb back over to our garden, my mother is waiting, pacing, panting. The smell of her cigarette wafts over the fence and gets up my nose. There are no crates on this side to help me over the fence, so I have no choice but to go through the flowers, doing irreparable damage.

I am sent to my room, and I am not allowed to go to school for the end of term. I have to help at home. I sit for many hours at the window and watch. The birds return the next morning, the flowers are replanted two days later by the nice lady with the jerk chicken, but it takes weeks before I hear the children back out playing in their own garden. When I hear them, I run to the window. The sun dances alongside their game and makes the water in the paddling pool sparkle like diamonds. Not once do they look towards my window. Not once do they ask me back to play. Not once do they realize that, according to my parents, we are moving again, this time because of me, because of them. I don't understand what is so wrong about playing with your neighbours together on a summer afternoon that causes us to be, as my father says, evicted. I cannot ask what that means, but staying home from school means I hear things. I learn what my parents teach me. First I learn we are moving, and then I learn the reason. They teach me that it's my fault for not doing as they told me to. Then after half a bottle of whisky – which I am called from my room to fetch from the kitchen cupboard and to pour for them, and their friends – they complain (and their friends nod) that it is the neighbours' fault for the state of this country; for not only taking jobs off my parents but for something called a petition that the 'black bitch' organised. I learn from my mother that the nice lady with the jerk chicken always wanted us out so her family from Jamaica can move in, and I am the one that helped her get us out. My mother said this and spat in the sink.

Lesson over, I am dismissed and I skulk away to the corner of my brother's room in turmoil. If I knew that my nice afternoon in the paddling pool, with laughter and lightness and so much jerk chicken over my face that I didn't care if I couldn't lick it all off, would result in my mother falling out with the neighbours and my father packing up the pram with a sigh; if I had known an afternoon's play would result in the things to come, including our hardly going to school for months, as we move from place to place, with ever-increasing impact, I wouldn't have opened the window. I would have turned my temptation back towards the wardrobe and continued to wonder what is inside there that I am not allowed to touch. I would have gaped and gaped at the wardrobe door with my mouth open until I got bored and walked away or opened it to find out. If I had known what was to come, that the next few months would be all my fault, I would have walked away. Instead I accepted an invitation from my neighbours and got a hard lesson about the niceties of other people and their houses. A real lesson on the highs and lows of a white girl being friends with black people in Hackney in the summer of 1979.

Black cabs, 1979

There is a taxi outside the house. I hear its funny taxi-cab engine ticking over. An angry man's voice. I look out the window of the bedroom, which I normally share with Mum and Dad, but because they both went out I slept on my own last night.

It's a black cab, one from the West End. Mum is standing on the pavement, swaying, ugly-looking with the drink, red shoes in her hand, the morning light doing her no favours, and the taxi driver is also out of his cab. He isn't happy:

'Pay the bloody fare, or I call the coppers.'

Mum is being all sweetness and light. She touches his arm. I flinch. He pushes it away. I relax a bit.

'Listen, one last chance, lady.' His hand is stretched out, palm up. 'Money.'

He looks her up and down. Mum is using her posh voice, the one she uses most of the time when men are around, and she is smiling through her red lipstick:

'I don't have the money. It was a tough night, you know?' A lowering of her eyes. A sideways movement of the hips. She smiles, speaks softly, kindly: 'You know, we can settle this another way.'

The taxi driver's face turns red with rage. He's so angry his nose is turning purple. He didn't like that.

'I'm calling the cops.'

Mum switches in an instant. Her back arches, she snarls, she turns towards the house. 'Awww fuck off. Ya all the same. Go fuck yerself.'

She turns back towards him and waves her red shoes in his face. He takes a step back, not sure he wants to deal with this. Her tights are ripped and her hair is not as perfect as it was when she went out last night. Even so, when the curtains of the neighbours across the street move, her back straightens, and she walks, with her hips swivelling, up the stairs, leaving the front door open behind her. The taxi driver is screaming in through the door, 'Give me my fucking money!' 'Fuck off, you cunt,' my mother screams back. She's on the stairs, effing and blinding to herself. The cab driver eventually gives up and leaves.

'Hope, where's your fuckin' father?' she shouts.

I leave the window and go downstairs to tell her he's not home yet. In no time at all, the cab driver is back, and a policeman is with him.

'Missus, you need to pay the cab driver.'

'Fuck off, he's a liar, I ain't been nowhere.'

The cab driver is screaming, my mother is screaming, the copper is trying to get my mother to pay up.

'Last chance. Pay the cab driver, or you're coming with me down the nick.'

'Who gives a fuck, do what ya want, I ain't paying that cunt.'

'Come on. Quietly now, you know the routine.'

'What about the kids?' my mother is screaming. 'Leave the kids on their own now, will ya? Hope! Look after your brothers. I've been nicked 'cos of that cunt's lies.'

I look at the copper, pleading with him in my head, for him to stop all this, just take her if that's what ya gonna do. He looks at me and says, 'Hope, I know you're a good girl, none of this is your fault.'

I start crying. I want him to be my dad, take me away from this hellhole called home. *Please, please, please*, I beg in my head.

'I'll be fine, mate, ta,' I say.

My mother is kicking and screaming at the copper, as he tries to take her away. She is hanging on to the banister. 'Fuck off!' she screams. The curtains across the road twitch again.

I put my hands over my ears. *Get out, get out, get out,* I say over and over in my head. *I hate you, I hate you,* over and over. My head is hurting real bad, the screaming and fighting continues, the copper calls for more coppers. I want to run to my bedroom, but don't want to leave my mum, and the confusing feelings overwhelm me. *Leave her alone,* I scream in my head. *Take her away,* in the next breath. More coppers arrive, bundle her up, and throw her in the back of the van. Without a look back, they all drive off.

2

SILVER CROSS PRAM

Moving again, 1979

We moved a lot when I was young. I'd see Dad, his tall, broad, well-built, smartly dressed frame pushing a Silver Cross pram containing all we owned. TV, suitcase, carpet, bottles, a few toys all piled precariously high. Dad scurrying down the road with my mum tottering behind him hauling my two younger brothers behind her – and I'd know. We were moving.

This time was different. I'd just gone back to school after the summer. School is round the corner from our house. The best thing about school is the lunch I get every day, except the weekends. So this morning, I didn't want to look out the classroom window just before lunch and see my family, and the pram, coming to get me. As they turn the corner into the street my school is on, a crowd of neighbours is shouting in their wake, as always seems to happen when we move. Their words follow my family down the road, not quite reaching the school gate, just like my family. Instead they stand on the other side of the road, waiting, smoking and drinking. I know the drill from when we used to collect Phillip from school. Now I go to school I see it how he sees it. I sink deeper in my seat, half under the desk, but I can still see them. They will stand there opposite the gate until my eldest brother, or the police, move them on round the corner and away from the school. I know I have to get there before the police come or I'll get lost.

Luckily we are never at a school long enough for my new friends to know who they are. Kids laugh at them:

'Check out the tinkers.'

'Look at what she's wearing.'

People cross the road rather than pass them. My family waits, smokes and swears, as if they've nothing else to do until the school bell rings. But this time Mum isn't there. My dad is struggling with the pram and my two younger brothers. I wait. I look at the clock on the wall, but I don't know what it says.

How long till the bell?

The teacher looks quickly at, and then away, from me. She looks out the window and tells us all to be quiet and get on with our work. She looks at me again with that look the shopkeeper has for me when I pass by.

What does that look mean? Oh, Dad! I can't do me letters now.

I watch Dad. He's standing, not smoking. Just staring. Then he starts playing with the boys. Hide and seek behind the pram. Running round it. Screaming with laughter.

As soon as the lesson is finished, I run. The school gates are open at lunchtime, and I run through them and the crowd of mothers waiting on this side of the road for their children. Dad is on the other side, also waiting. He's quiet again.

'Hi. Are we moving, Dad? Where's Mum? What's happened? Where are we going to live now, Dad?'

'Shut the fuck up and come on, Hope. Why always so many bloody questions? Never can take anything I tell ya, without bloody questions. Just move.'

We walk back the way we came, past the crowd of neighbours. We walk past our house, the door painted with letters I can't join up to form words yet. The colour of the paint is red, and the letters I do know. I say the letters one by one, so I will remember them when I ask Phillip to put the letters together. G–E–T. O–U–T.

We walk. Dad's head is held high, so ours are too. He is ignoring jeers of 'Good riddance!' that echo from dark doorways, and we fall into line, also pretending not to hear. An occasional, 'Poor neglected mites', or, 'So skinny. What kind of life is that for a child? You should be ashamed of yerself.'

We move in unison, tiny, grubby hands holding on to the pram in case we can't keep up. Doing all we can not to be left behind. Faces and eyes front, we all focus on the end of the road, walking, half running, beside Dad as he moves silently along the quieter backstreets of Hackney to a new home. Destination unknown to us kids, but we know Dad knows where we are going.

Dad's a foundling. He told me once he's a Barnardo's child. I often find him peddling stolen goods at the edge of a market, always well dressed, his bulky frame selling all sorts of stuff that bulges out of an old black suitcase, the pile ever decreasing as the day moves from dawn to dusk.

Phillip is always standing nearby, pretending not to be with Dad, while he watches like a hawk for any sign of the law. Sometimes, I stand in the shadows learning from Phillip and my dad. One day I hear a man say to my dad, 'You've turned peddling into an art form of survival.' So I know I am learning from the best. He sells what he can find, each hoard providing excitement the night before they go onto the street corner, with no licence and my eldest brother on the lookout.

I'm not sure my dad ever did any legal sort of work. I'm not sure he knew how. 'My job is looking after you lot and yer mum. It's a full-time profession to be proud of. Yer mum does very well.'

Living on the edge of life, wheeling and dealing whatever is available to him. Never wishing to attract attention. Always ensuring, when he can, that we are provided for. I love my dad – unlike my mother, he shows interest in me. He means well. In his own way, he tries to fulfil our wishes, if only through stealing.

As we walk, I count everyone and check everything. Dad said it was a responsibility helping him move, and I take this very seriously. I sink between the pram and the wall, beside my family, trying not to be seen by neighbours or friends, and then I check the pram to make sure Dad has remembered to pack everything of mine, my sleeping blanket and my Barbie doll with no arms. Yes, there she is. I can see her legs sticking up from the bottom of the pram. Next I count the family and go through their names. Me first, I am five and a half; then Jack, who is two and a bit, now sitting on Dad's shoulders as Dad pushes the pram. The pram wobbles. Jack should walk. Jack's named after nobody in particular, so next I count Harold. He's nearly four, and named after Dad's hero. Dad was very angry when someone called Harold Wilson resigned. Said everything would go to pot. I'm not sure where pot is, but apparently we are going there. Mum and Dad shout a lot about this country going to pot. I hope we aren't going there right now. Next I count Phillip. He's twelve years older than me. He can read AND write. He's named after the Queen's husband. Dad likes him because he says silly things, the Queen's husband that is, not my brother. My brother is very serious. But he is not here. I look back down the road to our broken house to see if he's following us.

Where is my brother? Where's Mum? Are they hurt? Oh shit, are they hurt?

'Dad?'

'Shut up, Hope.'

Will he be on his own? Will he find us? Maybe he's with Mum, or maybe she is away again. How far do we have to walk?

I catch the eye of my tiny three-year-old brother, his right hand steadying the load as he runs behind the pram. We are all proud to help Dad move. People looking, people averting their eyes. No chance of saying goodbye to my friends, though Dad says there's no point. Every time we move, Dad says they aren't my friends anymore: their mothers are the reason we had to move. There are a lot of people to blame, according to my mum. Once we've settled and got poor old Mum and Dad a drink, Mum will tell us tonight whose fault it is that we had to leave, who stuck their nose in and ruined her business. That black bitch, and this one, taking Dad's job off him. That confuses me, as Dad has never had a job, and there are no black dogs in our area, only a white funny-looking dog, with a fat nose. In any case, this move is the same but different. No Phillip. No Mum. Overnight my friends have decided not be my friend any more. I say 'Hi' as we pass, but they don't look at me as we walk down the street.

Where's Mum? Where's Phillip?

We walk, the illusion created by Dad's smart clothing, shattered. All I now know is we are evicted, forced out by my mother's behaviour. That sinking feeling from my throat to my stomach, the shame. Again. At that time I didn't know why we kept moving. But at least they took us with them.

Princess Lodge, 1979

The gates to the house are bigger than anything we have seen before. Red stone posts marking the gate – each twice the size of Dad. They are so big I have to lean all the way backwards to see the top. We walked here pushing the pram and now we stand, Dad, Harold, Jack and I, at the bottom of loads of concrete steps – looking up. I check the pram one final time, making sure nothing has dropped off along the way across Hackney to Bethnal Green. I have kept a close eye on the pram. Sometimes too close. I walked straight into it, twice! The first time it was not deliberate, but we all laughed at my silliness so the second time I did it deliberately, pretending to be Charlie Chaplin. We are here now, so my responsibility is over.

The house towers above us. It looks almost like a fairy castle in the books I've seen at school. I can't read the words yet, so I look at the pictures. All dirty pink stone, in big blocks, with huge windows where, for a moment, I think I see children staring out at us. It looks dirty, but I don't want to think about that as it spoils my fantasy. I like that there are flowers on some of the bushes, roses, pink and white. The sun shines. The sky is the blue of late summer, and I feel warm inside and out because Dad has taken us somewhere special.

I can count, so I count three big windows along the middle with two windowpanes in each window, each as high as a bus, nearly. This row is below the roof; the roof sticks out and there are another two windows sticking out of the roof – they only have one pane each, but they make it look almost like a castle. On the ground floor there are two big windows that stick out a bit from the house in a half square, and a bright yellow door. Despite being tired, we manage to jump in excitement.

'Wow! Dad, are we going to live there?'

'Yes, Hope, that is Princess Lodge. Your new home. Just for a bit. Other families live here too, it's such a big house.'

'Aw, Dad, it's great!'

'We will all have to share a room, but it'll be fine.'

'Dad? Are Mum and Phillip coming too?'

'Yer mum will be here tomorrow.'

A dark choking feeling rises from my stomach. I'd been looking forward to time on my own with Dad and the boys. Mum coming back – that will spoil things. He makes no mention of Phillip, and I know not to ask.

A week or two later, Jack and I are playing in the living room with two new friends who also stay at Princess Lodge. Until we arrived, they didn't know it was called Princess Lodge: they thought it was called something else. Dad can't be wrong as he brought us here. There are lots of rooms here that we cannot go into without an invitation. Families go into their own rooms, and then everyone can go into the communal rooms. In the living room, there is a big shutter, which goes up and down every morning. I learn to love the sound of the shutter rising. Behind it is what I now know to be called the 'tuck shop' which really means sweets and crisps to me and the other children.

When they first show us round, we just see most of the house from the big corridors and from the outside. We slide down the banister and get into trouble, we go up and down and down and up all the stairs and down the back-stairs to the kitchen. We play in the lift – first time I've ever seen one. This place is the biggest place I have ever been in with its own front door. The tower blocks in Hackney are big, but there are lots of front doors and small windows. Princess Lodge, once you are inside you are inside. You don't have to go out again. That's good because now the leaves are starting to turn orange and are beginning to fall down; it's getting colder, but the sun is still shining. The windows in the roof are known as the attic, and we cannot go there either. Here they keep the spare stuff. I'm not sure what spare stuff is exactly, but I do know the people who own this place must be very rich if they don't use every-thing they have, if they have some spare stuff that sits in the attic gathering dust.

There are fire exits on each floor. On our first day here we are shown them all by this man who says he's the manager. The living room is downstairs. It's a bit like a lounge, but one that all the families staying here can use. I play there in the daytime with my new friends and the adults sit in there at night.

My mum arrives the day after we do, just like Dad said she would. Every day we stay here she sweeps in and out of the living room, tottering on her stiletto heels and bare legs, asking me about the whereabouts of my fucking father, slamming the door behind her. She leaves a new atmosphere in the living room. My friends always stare in stunned silence at her wake. She leaves an air of perfume and alcohol behind that always makes me feel a bit sick. Every time, I wish she would take all of her out of the room with her.

Our bedroom is directly above the living room, and the tuck shop. Despite the size of the place, we can hear her shouting at him. I don't feel much like playing now. I want to look out the window and leave Jack and the two new friends we will not know for very long playing Snakes and Ladders. I sit in what I'm told is the bay window. I shut the heavy green curtains to make myself a den, as well as trying to block out the screaming taking place in the room above my head. My parents' fighting is overpowering the peaceful sounds of the house, like a whirlwind seeping into the walls and carpets, destroying the calm and rebuilding an unwanted and unstable atmosphere. I put my hands over my ears and watch the coming of autumn and the gathering clouds.

Poor Dad, he just wants to sleep. He's been up late with his friends. They couldn't go out to the pub as the doors of Princess Lodge shut at ten. When he put us to bed in the room we all now share, he told us for the first time in forever where he would be: 'Just downstairs.' If we need him, we should shout. He was off for a few tinnies and maybe some whisky with his new friends. He didn't want to leave us alone, but he'd had a hard day and it's only fair. He wants to make new friends as we have made new friends. I counted twenty families who live in this house, so hopefully Dad will find some new friends here. Each family has their own room and proper beds and sheets. I share a bed with Jack, which is OK because it is a bed, not a mattress, and we have a blanket that is thicker than the sheet we have at home. The sheets smell of fresh flowers, not piss, but that won't last long.

Oh no – I need to make sure the manager doesn't find out I piss me bed.

All the families will live here only for a little while, until they get sorted. Every one of Dad's mates talk about it being a sailor's hostel. 'What does that mean?' I ask them.

'Shut up, Hope, will ya?' Dad shouts.

When my new friend, finally, agrees my dad is right about the name of this place – Princess Lodge – she also has to have her dad be right about something, so in return she says her dad said Princess Lodge is for sailors with nowhere else to go. That confuses me a little, as sailors still have their boats, don't they? I must remember to ask Dad later. It's OK here. Only this is no longer our home. It is a room in a house with other people who don't have a house. The people who are still in their houses don't want any of us living at our house any more. Dad said they are all busybodies who should mind their own business. When Mum comes, I wonder what she will say about the old neighbours.

Not much as it turns out: she has a lot more to say about

Dad. He leaves after the row to go and get himself sorted. Mum sits the whole of the rest of the day in the living room, drinking. She too has found herself a new friend. The two of them sit there all day and drink. They are having a good time, laughing loudly and filling the room with smoke. Us kids do as we are told and fuck off. We go to play in the hall and on the stairs.

It's dark before Dad comes back. He calls us all to the kitchen and I can see from his face he is excited and pleased with himself. Mum cackles from the living room that she hopes he has brought more booze. With a raising of one eyebrow and a smile, he tries to persuade her to come see. We three kids perch on high kitchen stools, staring at the blue- and pink-striped plastic bag my dad has brought in. We stare in silence until she arrives. No one is brave enough to guess. Such ceremony, such excitement from my dad, attracts other people who stay here. We all wait in anticipation, even my mother. Dad has, as his good lady wife requested only yesterday, gone and got himself sorted, and here, before us, is the result. He always calls her that. I don't see what is good about having her as his wife.

He takes hold of one corner of the plastic bag, lifts, and shakes the contents out. With a rustle and a low thud, it lands on the table. A chicken. A whole chicken. For us. Dad is standing with his back straight, so proud. Mum forgets her new friend, who she has been hanging on to, and runs over to kiss Dad. Dad is even more proud. He throws both his arms round Mum and they kiss, like a proper snog. We kids take our cue and dance around the kitchen. Indian warriors whooping and dancing, our father has just made a killing, and brought home the bacon. Or in this case, chicken.

We dance and we laugh and we bow to the chicken and to our father, the chief, the head of the household, as we build up the excitement of the chicken and what it means for our tummies. We dance and we laugh, not noticing all the other families fading away in silence. We jump around delighted with ourselves, until we are exhausted from playing Indians, pretending Dad is the chief and Mum the squaw. We are all delighted that we don't need to pretend to play anymore. We all stop and stare. We check again in silence. The pink lump on the table is indeed real. It's a chicken. It's ours. Dinner. Tomorrow. Princess Lodge is already bringing good things.

Mum and Dad go to bed early. Saying stuff like they can't live without each other and that times are going to get better. Laughter, not fighting, come drifting down through the floorboards from the family room to the living room. We are allowed to stay up late, and Mum and Dad, for once, go to bed early.

We leave Princess Lodge in a hurry. A day of chaos. The next day the chicken had gone. We didn't eat any of it. It got stolen. Mum went mad. She stormed out, leaving us with Dad.

The fire alarm is screaming. Dad stops us sleeping in our nice warm beds, shakes us awake.

Me, Harold and Jack move from dreaming to a state of alertness with hardly a blink of an eye. Phillip isn't here just now. He did find us after a few days of our living in the Lodge, but he quite often stays somewhere else. We are awake now but my eyes are stinging. I want to shut them:

instead I rub them. That doesn't help either. It hurts to breathe. We all cough at the same time. The air feels dry, hot, burning the back of my throat; it tastes like burnt toast.

'Get up now. Fire! Get up. Hope, help your brothers. Throw everything in this. Pack. Quick.'

It's dark. Dad hasn't switched on the light, but the room doesn't feel right, and our eyes and ears confirm our suspicions. Even through the darkness I can see smoke winding its way through the floorboards, entering the room, announcing its arrival. The heat is squeezing between my toes and caressing the sides of my feet. The smell of burning seeps into my skin as it rises up to and into my nose, filling every pore. A woman's scream travels from the top of the stairs with the oak banister that we slide down every day, through our door. We hear the scream and it passes through our bones. Despite the warmth in the room, I shiver. Other bedroom doors are opening all at once with a collective squeak, then as footsteps move towards the stairs they slam shut by themselves. Footsteps that pass our room, then down the stairs. People and their feet moving quickly, accompanied by 'Oh my God!' and 'Come on! Come on!'

The panic, the chaos of other people, begins to crawl under our own skins. Harold, who never cries, chooses this moment to start. I try to be brave, as we shove what belongs to us into the cases. The smoke we can smell, the fear we acknowledge, but we focus on the job Dad has asked us to do. Other people's reactions to the fire creep under our door, reach us as we scramble, filling the Silver Cross pram with our belongings, as it stands next to our beds, a gaping mouth awaiting her cargo.

'Grab everything you can. Put this over your face.'

The door opens and the warden appears. He looks viciously towards my dad.

'What are you doing? Get out. Now. Walk carefully. Leave the bloody pram and cases.'

Running, we half ignore the order and drag our cases, but leave the pram. I am holding my doll, which has no arms, in my right hand, and my case is being dragged by the left. We are all calm. We don't question my father's judgement, and know we have to take what we can with us, or all hell will break loose. We move downstairs, outside. To safety. A fire engine has arrived. Firemen rushing around. One man is on the radio calling for more fire engines, for support. Another directs us away from the building:

'Over there, at the bottom of the drive.'

This time, we do as commanded and we follow the direction of his pointing finger.

'Is everyone out?'

It's a tired voice that no one answers. We stand still, not knowing the answer, sleep having being rudely interrupted, unaware of the enormity of the situation. Then as we rub our smoke-filled eyes, coughing, holding our bed sheets around us, carrying our bags, we notice the ground is orange, and long shadows are created. I look up: all the residents are standing watching Princess Lodge. They stand with blank faces, each wearing all they own, or holding all they could carry. Adults, children, the warden. All looking the same way. I can feel the heat on the side of my head, so I turn to see what they are watching. Princess Lodge is engulfed. The flames lick the side of the second floor, up the inside of the downstairs windows, enjoying their meal.

Flames leap into the night sky. Despite the fire, it's cold. There are no clouds and Jack Frost is already dancing on the tips of the leaves that in the last week I have watched turn from green to red and orange.

My eyes widen as fear once again grips me.

Where is my mum?

I stare and stare at the house. The flames have now reached our bedroom: an almighty thunderous noise signals the end of our room. I look around again for my mother. She is not here. I don't understand: before I went to sleep, I heard her. Shouting, drunk, still trying to find out who had stolen our chicken. I am afraid of the answer, afraid to ask. I swallow hard, my throat hurts, and I take my dad's hand. He looks down at me, a small sad smile, so I pluck courage out of the air.

'Dad, where is Mum?'

'She is OK. Don't worry, Hope, we'll find her. She's gone to a friend's. Everyone got out.'

The family who live in the room across the hall from ours, hear my dad say this and turn their heads. The man – whose name I don't know, but I do know he drinks with my mum and dad downstairs in Princess Lodge – walks over, looks my dad in the eye and spits on the ground, right next to my blackened bare feet and Dad's shoes. Dad does nothing. He just stands and stares back, gripping my hand tighter. The man walks away but his eyes stay sharply on Dad. I don't like how he is looking, so I stare at the ground, at the spit as it trickles towards Dad. I want to tell Dad that the spit is coming, but I don't. I feel the heat of the fire reaching us and I see, for the first time, the top of my dad's shoes aren't attached to the bottom part. There is a hole where there should be stitching.

My dad shifts from foot to foot. I know that without Mum he doesn't know what to do. Harold and Jack each grab one of Dad's legs, unable to take their eyes off the fire. Jack is in the middle between Dad and me. Dad's arm is over Jack's head, still holding my hand. I move closer into Jack, pushing him against my dad. We stand there for a bit, tight as thieves, until the flames snake through the upstairs windows and bite on the overhanging roof, where the swallows nest and where we watched for hours trying to spot the chicks as they strained out of the nest to be fed. I look to the ends of the flames.

The mummy and daddy swallows are darting to and fro, between the flames, frantically trying to get to their nest. They look scared but determined. I can see them crying out in distress. I know what this means. The baby swallows, three of them, cannot yet fly. I watch the parents swoop towards the heat, then dart away from the flames. With a final low swoop, a bow at the end of the show, they both disappear into the night sky, alone but together. A tear escapes down my face; I wipe my nose with the back of my free hand and find it comes away covered not only in snot, but soot and tears. The baby swallows will be engulfed by the lapping, cracking flames.

We stand like this until we hear a new set of sirens in the distance, heading our way. As if awoken from a trance, Dad moves slightly, gently releasing my hand and shaking the boys off his leg. He picks up his suitcase in silence. He motions with his head for us to do the same. In turn, we pick up our pieces of luggage and we turn away from the fire. We follow our dad as he walks through the majestic gates, without looking back or saying a word.

We walk down the road, managing as best we can with the bags but without the Silver Cross pram or Mum to help us. As the sirens get louder, Dad pushes us into the bushes, just before the emergency services turn the corner into our street. For a moment, Harold, Jack and Dad's faces are lit up by the yellow and blue flashing lights. The boys are fascinated, but my dad is obviously thinking. We crouch there for some time, unseen, and long after four more fire engines and two police cars career towards Princess Lodge. I get cramp and need to pee.

'Why we hiding from the firemen, Dad?'

'Well, Hope, the thing is your mother, your mum, well she . . .'

He rubs his face as if to rub something out of his head. When he speaks, it comes out all at once as fast as the fire engines that passed. I almost don't hear him right.

'Those guys back there, they were saying yer mum set fire to the curtains. Because of the chicken, someone stole the chicken. The warden was saying all sorts of stuff about the way she . . . well . . . about being a mother. That's why she ran, through the fire escape and away. We had to go before the police came.'

He is sitting in the bushes with us, knees skyward, bottom on the ground, and his arms are around his knees. He bends his head and rubs his eyes with one hand, slowly back and forth, pressing in at the sides of his head, pushing the pressure all out. I stand, as much as I can, and step through a bush, the twigs springing back onto my leg with a sharp whack, and I give him a hug. We crouch there, me patting his back with tiny hands, my face nuzzled into his neck, until I feel him breathe in as he straightens his back. As he pushes his way out to the road, he breaks the silence with:

'Come on, kids, no point in sitting here all night. Who's for a midnight adventure? Let's go and find your mum.'

I yawn and wearily stand. We all manoeuvre our way out of the bushes, a task more difficult than going in. My dad marches down the road walking funny – he says like Charlie Chaplin – and singing. He makes us giggle and we trot after him. *He's my dad.* He will follow my mum anywhere, without question. I, in turn, follow him.

Letter to Lily

January 2011

Dear Lily,

As your nana, it is difficult for me to balance the need to protect you, to keep you safe, with my ability to warn you away from strangers. The kindness of strangers helped us kids survive. This diverse community seemed to understand family values better than we did, which was ironic given my mum's entrenched racism. It's they who took me in, looked out for us. I don't think the kind folk of Hackney thought we had a home at all. So wild and free, we seemed to be 'those street kids'. Cheeky smiles would inspire people from a couple of streets down to make us brown bread and jam sandwiches. We thought they must be so rich to have brown bread! I always smiled to myself when I made them for your mum and uncle as they grew up.

The kebab shop always gave us extra salad, even though we never asked. Jerk chicken appeared from the people next door before my mother and racism stepped in. People seemed to like to feed us, when they could.

During the winter of '79, we were moving from house to house, never staying more than a few sleeps. Mum was away a lot and it must have been tough for Dad to survive. There were no jobs, no one had any cash. He was drinking when he could. I missed a lot of school, and as far as I remember no social worker came to where we were staying. Dad must have gone to them.

We moved to lots of bed and breakfasts in Finsbury Park, and without my mum around I could speak to the neighbours who lived in the room below us.

The first time I see her, she is playing outside on the road in front of the B&B. We have only been here a couple of days. I stand on the steps, one foot on one step and one on the other, holding on to the big grey stone wall, and I count the chips out of the concrete, with one eye on her.

She has drawn a hopscotch game, and without saying anything to each other we just end up playing together.

She is so *exotic*.

This is a word I heard from the man at the market talking about pineapples and coconuts. I stole a pineapple and we had it for breakfast. It tasted sharp.

She has gold-coloured bangles on her wrists, loads of them.

'They are so cool!'

She nods. She has big brown eyes and dark olive skin, perfect skin. I find out that she lives in the room below me.

After this first meeting, I knock on her door often, to play with my first real friend. I don't tell my dad about my new friend, but I feel bad about it 'cos I really want to tell him how great she is. Her dad is also like mine, lovely. Then again, he is also very different from my dad. Her dad cooks.

The family lets me in when she is there, and even when she isn't. They are very kind. The spice smell that comes from their room attracts me and increases my curiosity. I knock, I go in, I play with a baby. Just like in our room, there never seems to be a mum. Unlike our room, theirs is calm, quiet, a haven from the world outside. Worlds apart in so many ways, yet they couldn't have been kinder.

'Come in, come in, Hope. Help me here.'

'What's that you're doing?'

'Making chapattis, here take this ... stir this ... cook this ...'

Helping out in the kitchen corner – over a Calor gas open flame cooker with two rings – is fun. They laugh and are patient with my endless questions, which never seem to disturb them.

'Why do you eat with your hands? What is this spice? What does that do? Are you allowed a cooker in the room? What are you making?'

Even when I make a mess trying to help them cook, they smile and laugh with me. When I don't have a clue, they calmly show me a better way. When I get upset that I make such a mess kneading the flour dough for chapattis, the older Indian girl just wipes down my top, smiles and comforts me.

Everything I do is met with a warm smile, and when we sit down to dinner, they just assume I will eat with them. An open palm, covered in henna, gently sweeps – directing me from the gas stove to sit on the floor, to my place, which is already set. They always seem to eat on the floor, in a big circle. In our room, we just sit on our beds all squashed together, dropping food on the covers.

It's sad to me now, that such experiences couldn't have been shared with my dad. I wanted him to be curious, to have such a calm, wise friend – and for him to have been able to look after us. As a parent, I am sad he did not experience the joy of sitting silently looking at his sleeping children, or looking at you, my grandchild, as you sleep in a cot next to me. How he missed out on so much happiness; on helping us kids grow up properly. He did not experience two very different things: the sense of satisfaction that comes from cooking for your family; or the many cultures that were around us at that time. He never appreciated that we are all connected, we are just trying to survive.

To this day, Lily, your mum will tell you that I can't stand any form of discrimination. I am now fighting for vulnerable people's rights, so they are able to live better lives. I am proud that your mum also shares these values.

More to come soon, Lily.

I love you,

Nana

3

VISITORS

Grandma, 1980

We've recently moved into our new house on Hamilton Street. Jack and I are waiting, ready to be on our best behaviour.

I see them first, coming round the corner, so I run inside and shout:

'They're 'ere.' I rush back outside.

When they arrive at the house, they are still walking in a line and in the order I saw them in when they first turned the corner into our street.

Leading is my grandma, not wearing her flowery pinny today, but she is wearing a hat. She has a stern face, looking like she can smell something nasty, with her lips all curled up. Mum always said it's because my grandma is from South London, so she looks down on the East Londoners, even us. Following are my auntie and uncle. They are both tall and have kind-looking faces. They are both smiling and when they get closer I can see it's not just smiles with their mouths, it is with their eyes as well.

I watch as they walk down the street, looking at each Victorian terraced house, at the numbers on the doors, to read number 26. When they get to number 18, I stop playing, right in the middle of my game of hopscotch, to tell my mum that the moment has finally come.

In response to my shouting, Dad rushes round the living room and smoothes his hair flat, while Mum stands us all to attention behind the front door in the hall.

Mum's there at the door before the bell rings. Lucky she is, otherwise they'll know it doesn't work. Smiling at the relatives who visit for the first time, Mum is speaking all posh, and I want to laugh, as she sounds funny, but I don't. She ushers them into the living room. They sit staring at each other. Grandma's eyes are moving around the room slowly, taking everything in.

Is that a flinch?

We knew they were coming. This morning, Dad took a face cloth to our faces, and said: 'Scrub a dub dub!' He even washed inside our ears. Told us not to go out to play today. But we did, just outside the front door, though. He didn't notice because he was tidying the house some more. He's also been doing that all week, especially the living room. He's been cleaning and Mum's been shouting.

We've been told not to let the visitors go anywhere else in the house, and to 'Say nuffink about our friends coming round to the house, or that they drink.'

We know that already, because Mum and Dad tell us this most days – before we go to school, before we go out to play, and before they go out to the pub.

This day, we are rewarded with a bag of sweets from my auntie. Pick 'n' Mix, from Woolworths.

We stand for ages as Auntie asks questions about school and about living with Mum and Dad. She asks me, but Mum answers everything. I don't know how Mum knows so much about my school. She knows I don't go often, 'cos we are always moving. But she answers for me, and as we stand waiting to eat our sweets, I learn that Dad has got Harold and me into the school at the end of the road. I start next week.

Mum explains, 'Everything else is going well, now we are settled.' Her smile is there, but her stare is cold.

'That's nice,' my aunt responds, nodding slowly. Like she is trying to understand something. The air seems to get heavier in the room.

I'm bored. I start to pick another hole in the sofa. Dad taps my hand away, so I just stand staring at my grandma, who doesn't say much and whose lips are thin and unsmiling.

Hurry up. I want to get out to eat the sweets. What's the point of givin' us sweets if we have to wait to eat them? Go. Go. Hurry up!

After a while, and with no warning, my grandma tells my aunt and uncle, 'Well. We'd better be going then.'

'Yes, all right then.' A bit quick there, Mum, I think.

So they leave.

I run out into the street, counting, skipping and jumping, playing hopscotch again, but this time with the best-looking sweets in Hackney. I feel special.

That evening, I am still playing out the front, leaving my mum and dad drinking much quicker than normal, when I see some of Mum's men friends come out from the alley that runs up the side of our house. These two always have a shopping trolley with them. It is blue. They always have sweets for us, and drink for Mum and Dad. I don't want their dirty sweets, and in my head comes the usual chant: 'Die, you dirty old man. Die, you dirty old man.' Over and over it plays, every time they come round and hand out sweeties.

When they leave, Dad has some money. As he sometimes does when they get money, he sends us off to Kentucky Fried Chicken, my favourite shop. Finger lickin' never felt so good.

Mum and Dad have a furious argument that night about Grandma and Auntie and Uncle coming there. Mum is upset, saying over and over, 'How could my own mum kick me out when I got pregnant at seventeen, and make me give my baby away? Beautiful she was. Horrible bastard, my dad. Thank fuck he's dead and buried.'

No wonder my dad knocks back the hard stuff, putting up with her. I don't know who my mum's dad was, but I bet he drank too, with her around. He's better off dead. Shame he was dead before I was born. A granddad sounds OK. Doesn't really bother me though. Moaning cow, it shouldn't bother her either, 'cos it is done now.

I've no idea why the visitors came. It was the last time I ever saw my aunt and uncle. Grandma never came to visit us again.

Freezers, 1981

Two of the many practical things my dad is good at, are getting food without money and making lettuce sandwiches, with salt.

Today we are, according to my dad, 'on a special

mission'. Mum and Dad are wandering up and down the shop, looking at stuff, while I look for the chance to steal burgers. I know where they are, and I know what to do.

I have to wait until Mum and Dad are near the till, distracting the man behind the counter, who according to my mum, can afford to let us have this stuff for free. She calls him a 'bloody Paki', which is probably why she doesn't ask him to give us the food directly, and I have to steal it.

I wander up and down in front of the freezers, and the burgers are staring out at me. I've one eye on Mum and Dad, who are almost at the counter, and I hear them making a racket. That is the sign I am waiting for. Quick as a flash, I open the door, grab the burgers, turn away from the counter and shove the packet up my jumper. Walking slowly, I count the steps, one, two three, four . . . I look up.

I've got them, hurrah! Burgers for tea!

Proud as punch, I walk towards the door. I can see Mum and Dad have already left the shop and are standing on the other side of the road, where Harold and Jack were left to wait and look out for any coppers coming. Three more steps across the shop. The burgers are very cold up my jumper, but I have them.

Burgers for tea! Not just lettuce in the sandwiches but burgers too!

My mouth is dripping with saliva. It's cold 'cos it's almost winter, and the burgers are burning a cold patch on my tummy.

I have them!

A couple more steps and I will be at the door. One, two . . . three, my foot is outside the shop.

I've done it! Dad'll be so pleased with me. He taught me right!

A hand on my shoulder. My mouth dries up, quickly. My parents and brothers disappear from view, like a magic trick.

'Come on. I've been watching you. Hand them over.'

'What?' All wide-eyed and innocent, turning on my trademark cheeky smile.

'The burgers, the ones up your jumper, come on, give them back.'

Shit. I am in trouble now.

My family's gone. Me on my own facing the man I know I've just stolen from, even though he can afford it.

I pull the burgers out from under my jumper. I throw them on the ground. I feel a clip round the ear.

'Get out of here, and don't let me see you in here again!'

I run and run until I am breathless and catch up with my parents.

'Thought I was a goner there, Dad. Sorry I didn't get the burgers.'

I am not sure he hears me as they have already turned into the pub, leaving me, Harold and Jack standing outside, looking at the door. We kick around for a bit, waiting for them to come out. They don't. We make our own way home, each of us stopping ourselves dreaming of the burgers I lost.

Barbie, 1981

Sitting on the steps outside our house, in all weathers, is where I always wait for my dad. Biting my nails, playing with the broken Barbie I got for my fifth birthday, scraping the toes of my already worn shoes on the concrete. Looking, hoping he will come home today with something for the house, or even better, something for me!

I love Barbie and stand staring at her and Ken in the windows of the shops in Hackney. Their clothes, their hair, their perfect life. Barbie also has Ken. I stand there often with broken Barbie. We both try to talk to perfect Barbie until we are chased away, dreaming, wanting, willing them to break out of their boxes and the shop, imagining them coming home, with us.

Oh how I want my very own Barbie, with her own wardrobe and lots of pretty clothes. How I want to dress you.

I see my dad at the same time he sees me. He is carrying a lot of pink things.

'Hope, Hope, come help me, Hope!'

I run towards him, not sure what the panic is. When I get there I feel my eyes widen. In his arms are Barbie legs and Barbie arms, all joined by a Barbie body. Best of all he is carrying a Barbie wardrobe stuffed full of Barbie clothes. I stare in silence. Dad laughs.

'Grab a hold of these, girl, these are for you!'

I totter back to the front steps, staring, disbelieving. I place everything carefully on the top step and lay them all out. There are skirts and blouses, and trousers. Shoes and hats. Barbie has her own wardrobe, complete with little hangers. I've seen them in Woolies, so I set it up and start placing the clothes inside. I fold them all neatly, and hang clothes on some of the few precious hangers, examining the sewing and the patterns, all whites, pinks, browns and reds. Then I reorganise them all again, spending hours living in an imaginary Barbie world. I am so happy.

Barbie, my own Barbie.

I stroke her hair.

'Where, Dad, where, how?'

He is beaming. 'A skip, Hope, round the corner. You will never guess but someone is throwin' them out . . . there's more, ya know, there's more!'

Before I can reply, he's off, round the corner. It's all I can do to take my eyes off this tall hero of mine. This smartly dressed, well-built man was off to fulfil my dreams.

Barbie.

He returns and I run towards him, looking back to check on my precious hoard.

'Barbie's horse, more clothes, hairbrush and clips and a Barbie handbag! Oh, Dad, thanks, Dad, thanks, thanks. WOW. It's a Barbie, Dad!'

Laughing, he sits down next to me and we explore the loot. My chest all puffed up with delight and his with pride.

'Look. Look, Dad, look at this!'

The tiny clothes, the tiny hangers. I sort them for hours and hours, staying on the front step until after dark. My dad has done this, for me. For weeks, I play at tidying up the wardrobe, having Barbie try on all her different outfits.

Absolute heaven.

4

RHUBARB AND REBATES

Rhubarb, 1981

The weather has turned a bit colder today, so to help keep warm I am running. I like running. Jack and Harold are just about keeping up behind me. Up Stoke Newington High Street, grabbing a couple of apples from the stalls on the way, down Church Street and into Abney Park Cemetery, one of our favourite places to play. It's nearly the end of the summer holidays, so we don't get a regular meal. But I try to combine play with the boys and finding food. The guys who sit drinking all day, every day, wave as I go past.

They're funny sometimes; other times they can be really scary. The women are always the worst drunks, cursing and screaming at the men. They accuse them all of nicking their drinks. My mum calls them tramps, but they are my friends. I don't like it when the tramps fight, though. It can be men on men, woman on woman, or both! One great big fight. Today they are all in a good mood.

We all wave back, exchanging greetings. We have to pass back this way as they may have a few pennies for us later. The cemetery is like a jungle.

I think about what we will play today. *Tag? Hide and seek?* My tummy is sore. *Don't be hungry, forget about being hungry. It's Thursday, so we have only four more days to go until Monday money.*

Things at home are getting worse and worse, and my tummy is always sore now, morning to night. Jack and Harold complain of sore tummies too.

I do what I can.

We arrive at the big black gates, and all stop to catch our breath. Quietly, respectfully, we walk through the first part of the cemetery, past the gravestones none of us can read, to the middle jungle where we let loose. Whoops of laughter, count to ten and hide and seek.

'Coming to get ya!'

We hunt, we search, we laugh together, forgetting the reality of living. Enjoying ourselves among the dead.

When the light starts to fade, I call my brothers together again.

'Right, off to the treasure hunt, boys.'

We search right up to the edge of the walls. We go round trees and look under bushes. A cry: 'I've found it!' from one of us.

Each rushes over to stare at our prize: rhubarb!

We still play this game of 'hunt the rhubarb' even though we know exactly where it grows. Each time, we try to recapture the feelings we had the first time we stumbled across this crop. We found it because I tripped on a tree root, and from the cemetery floor looked up at the majestic green leaves that seemed bent towards me in welcome; purple stalks and faint green lines running up them, enticing us to pick them.

Each detail of the treasure hunt will fill me with pleasure for many years, until sadness replaces the feeling in later years, when I realise that finding food should have been an adventure, an add-on to childhood, not a necessity or a lesson in resourceful survival.

Rebate, 1982

I have a bike. A brand new bike. It is not stolen. My dad bought it. It got delivered this morning. I'm riding it down the road, round corners as fast as I can. It didn't take me long to learn how to ride this pink bike with a basket on the front. My brother has one too, though his one came a few days ago.

Dad has been telling us for weeks, in a higher voice than suits his frame, 'I'm going to get a lot of money soon, people!'

I hear him telling Mum, over and over: 'Can you fuckin' believe it? We haven't been getting the right money for years. The bastards have been short paying me benefits. Imagine that, all this fuckin' time. What did they call it, the "winter of discontent" all that fuckin' time. I'll give you discontent, no wonder we've been struggling for years, unable to make ends meet. The bastards weren't fuckin' paying us right. If it wasn't for that cunt of a social worker we wouldn't know. Better stop calling her that, ha ha! She's maybe not so bad after all. She says they owe me a lot of money, ya know, a lot of money. That money's mine. I'm entitled. What's that, it's coming soon, yeah, soon.'

What are benefits? Must be something to do with Dad not getting the right money and maybe it's something to do with Mondays.

Who cares? My mum and dad are dancing in the living room. They now like the social worker. They aren't drinking in the kitchen every hour of the day. Dad tickles my tummy, telling me we are going to be rich. Excitement from the adults and disbelief from their offspring fill the different rooms in the house.

While Dad waltzes Mum around the house, I speak with Harold about it in the kitchen. Both of us agree that it's maybe not true. The more Dad speaks about the 'backdated money', the more we want to believe him, but we just can't. A lifetime of broken promises, unfulfilled wishes and tears of disappointment means that at seven and six years old respectively, we both think of our dad as lying. We are waiting for the day he admits the money isn't coming, the one when he lets us all down, again. We know there is no money, no £700 pounds he keeps on about. Better to know that now, so when he admits it we won't cry.

Three sleeps he has gone on about the money, then another three sleeps. I am convinced he is lying, and I'm trying to work out what to tell Jack when we find out the truth. This morning Mum and Dad made me a cup of tea. We all sat down.

'Hope, stay in today, yeah? There are two surprises coming, for your brothers. You gotta be here to get them, OK?'

I don't believe you. Why are you lying to me? Daddy, please don't lie. I don't like it.

I am sitting at the window. I've been waiting a long time

now. Waiting, waiting, waiting. I pace up and down, move from seat to seat, go from room to room. My hands are being rubbed together, slowly at first, then faster and faster as I get increasingly anxious. I know they are lying to us.

Why are they lying to us? My brothers know they're not getting any surprises, it's so unfair. Unfair.

I stamp my feet in anger, let out a number of 'grrrr' noises, all in frustration. I hit a cushion, then sit down and cuddle myself. Wishing, wishing, dreaming my life was somewhere else. I munch through a lettuce sandwich Dad made me this morning, and drink water from the tap. I try to hold back the tears that come with each bite. I curse the unfairness of my life, how often we are let down, feel the intensity of hate building up within me. I focus on my stupidity. Even though I said I wouldn't, I do wish it's true. Even though all along I'm telling myself it just can't be, I secretly hope it can be. I wait and wait at home. I hit my legs with my fists to try and release the pain inside me. The day seems like it's stretching on forever. Waiting in for the doorbell to ring.

There is a knock on the door. I run to open it. I stop, as my breathing has gone a bit funny. I'm preparing myself again for disappointment. I open the door, pop my head out and there he is, a tall delivery man, in a uniform, and he is holding a bike and a box of Action Men, just like the ones we have seen on the TV.

A bike, Action Men. Oh! Daddy! Daddy!

I scream, 'Dad was telling the truth!'

I jump with joy and the boys come running.

'Presents are here! A bike, a Chopper bike! Action Men, just like on the telly!'

The delivery man is laughing with us, enjoying our surprise. I still haven't signed the paper he is holding. I am jumping, my brothers are touching their presents, three pairs of young eyes full of excitement are jumping up and down with true happiness.

New toys, and a kept promise from my dad.

My parents arrive home that evening, the booze bar in the living room fully stocked, and carrying Kentucky Fried Chicken. There is a lot of laugher in the house because of what Dad calls his windfall. We all play together, even Mum and Dad, everyone enjoying the boys' toys. As we play I begin to wonder:

Is there anything for me?

I go to sleep not knowing, trying to tell myself that the fact Dad kept his promise to the boys is enough. Hoping there will be something for me.

Waking late, to Mum and Dad busy in the kitchen, I kick my heels waiting once again.

They haven't told me. Maybe I won't get anything after all, more proof they don't love me as much as the boys.

Late afternoon, and I still don't know if and when I am getting anything. Mum and Dad are in the kitchen with the two men who are brothers and come round every so often, with their shopping trolley following behind like a dog. The chant in my head begins again, 'Die, you dirty old man. Die, you dirty old man.' Maybe if I say it enough they will die on their way home, get knocked over by a number 73 bus.

They are all laughing. I am standing in the hall, watching, waiting, working up the courage to go and ask for what I want, before they send me away. I kick the banister in boredom and frustration; I hang off it, swinging from side to side. My mother laughs. I cannot wait any more.

'Dad?'

'What do you want, Hope?' My father's voice is friendly, happy. The two fat old brothers are across the table from each other; both are staring at my mother, who has her back to me. My father, also facing my mother, looks past her at me standing in the door.

'Come in. Come in, Hope, tell yer old dad what's going on.'

I see the booze stacked up on the table. There is normally no more than a half-empty bottle in the house at the most. I know 'cos I have to serve them and their friends drinks from the stash in the living room. Now the bar is full, and this gives me courage. I take my chance.

'Dad?'

'What's up, Hope?'

'Can I 'ave a bike too, Dad?' The words have been trapped since I first thought of them last night. They have been held in under pressure, waiting for the right time. Now I am here asking for what I want, the words are released, they rush out. 'A pink bike, with a basket? A . . . a basket on the front?'

Now I've finished speaking, the room is silent. Everyone is staring at my dad, waiting for an answer.

'Of course you can, Hope. Of course you can. Now off ya go, we're busy.'

There is a collective sigh as I leave the room. I hear my mum:

'That girl does me 'ead in.'

* * *

I'm riding my bike now. It's pink with a basket on the front. It even has a bell. Ting. Ting.

It's the most beautiful thing I have ever owned, but that doesn't stop me riding it. The wind in my hair makes my eyes water. I cycle round Hackney, through London Fields, down Morning Lane, through the churchyard, down to Homerton Hospital, round the back down Graham Road and down to Stoke Newington, past Stokie Nick, waving as I go. I spend my days stuck to the seat of this bike, exploring Hackney like never before. Without a care I go. What a scoop we have had with this dosh. The thrill! I love this bike and I love my dad for getting it for me. I travel, I swoosh past shops, screaming at all who see my adventure, and laughing at neighbours, making them all turn to look at me as I go. I am so excited it takes me a while to notice things are changing at home.

My parents seem to be more drunk than normal. The arguments between them are increasing in intensity, still defined by screaming and shouting, but they seem louder. A crash and a bang as Mum throws another chipped mug at my dad's head; Dad screaming as she gets hold of his hair, scratching and punching him. Her feet make a lot of noise for the size of them, as she clumps up the stairs in anger to her bed. She spends an increasing number of days there. She appears every so often for a drink and to pick up the magazines Dad buys her and leaves outside the bedroom door. She is still effing and blinding, expressing her unhappiness, holding the house to ransom under her storm.

I don't understand it. Mum's not happy, even when we are rich!

We eat our KFC, which Dad buys us, like he has every

day since the money came and which he will buy until the money runs out. We eat, as we hear her calling out for more booze, for more this and that. Dad jumps up to her call, runs up to her, placates her. Peace for all of five minutes until she starts again and Dad tries to cosy up to Mum, tries to make her get out of bed, tries to make her happy.

Mum's coming home, 1982

Mum is away again without any warning. One day she is there, then she isn't. This week the social worker has told me there's a place I can go and play 'without the responsibility of your brothers, on your own, time for yourself'. I am not sure what she means, as I like being with my brothers. I don't like leaving them on their own. But she tells me they will be OK, she will 'sort something out', so I decide to give the place a go. This place is colourful and it's called a Project. Project 55. It's brilliant! The staff tell me it's an old fire station and that makes it even more exciting than the exciting it was before.

I have such fond memories of these six months, going there. We ran around the room, a number of kids, just like me. I liked the project workers, they knew about Mum being in prison and I could talk to them a little bit of what it was like to be at home. Five Wednesdays after I started, when it was really, really cold, I knew my mum was coming out of prison, but on the day she was coming home, I still went to the project. I liked it that much, and it was warm. It had been an 'unusually bad winter' and Dad hadn't always been able to have the gas fire on, so we didn't have hot water. That was another reason for going to the project that night, some warmth.

'I gotta go on time today. Mum's coming home tonight.'

'OK, Hope, off you go. Have you had a sandwich already?'

'Yes, thanks.' I walked out the door, warm full of sausage sandwich and with lots of lovely thoughts in my head about the big hug and warm greeting my mum would give me when I got home.

For twelve weeks, Dad has been drunk, wishing my mum was there.

'I miss yer mum, why isn't she 'ere? Ah, not long now till she comes 'ome . . . Shit, why did she have to get caught, she should be 'ere, wi' me.'

Now she is coming home, he will stop all that nonsense and things will be different this time. At the end of my road, I look down the street. The lights are on in the bay windows of our house, which means she must be home. I race down the slabs, past all the Victorian terraced houses with tidy gardens and curtains in the front room, full of excitement and a smile on my face that is so big you could shove two gobstoppers in at the same time.

She's home, she's home!

I fly up the steps two at a time. As soon as I open the front door, Tom Jones deflates me a little. That music means one thing. All is not well. I try to believe otherwise. Once again, in my head, I see, I imagine, a happy greeting, that all is going to be different this time.

'Mummy, Mum?'

'In here, Hope.' It's Dad who replies.

I burst into the living room, the door swinging open so hard that the handle hits the wall and a bit of plaster trickles to the floor.

Mum is sitting on the armchair, shoulders slumped forward, with a smile that is turned upside down. A drink is being slowly twisted around in her hand, in time to the music. Nothing in her says there is an ounce of happiness at her being home, at her seeing me.

I step forward. Slowly.

'Mum?' My arms raise a couple of inches, hoping she will respond with a hug.

'Where the fuck were you when I came home? I had a fuckin' terrible time in prison, the house is a fuckin' mess and you're out playin' when I get back. Why weren't you 'ere?'

The snarl, the self-pitying, the attention required, the focus on the glass rather than me as she spat this out, did its job. Without any hope of being wrapped in my mother's arms, the top of my head being kissed, the guilt starts in my tummy and arrives at the front of my head. What is not happening is my mum telling me she missed me, my brothers, my dad. *I missed you, I missed you.*

'Don't give her a hard time, luv, she was at 'er project.'

'I don't fuckin' care, she should 'ave been 'ere. The house is a bloody mess.'

'Sorry, Mum, I shouldn't have gone to the Project.'

'No, you bloody well shouldn't. Don't you know the sacrifices I make to put food in yer mouth? I swapped a bar of chocolate with the slag I shared me cell with, so you could have some shampoo. Over there on the table, go on have it! I go to prison for ya, and when I get home, you are at a bloody project.'

I am staring at my mum, confused and scared. I back off: the squeaky floorboard greets me.

How did she go to prison for me? I hate her. I hate her. I hate her.

Her voice echoes round the house, giving my dad a hard time, my dad taking it, his head getting lower and lower.

'I had a terrible time in Holloway, and this is the thanks I get.'

'I tried, I did try, luv.'

'I try to get money for the family, and what happens, none of you fuckin' care . . . You all abandon me when I come home. Terrible time . . .'

I close the door on her moroseness, sit on the stairs and let the guilt – at my not being there when she came home, about the way she is speaking to my dad because I was late – overwhelm me.

5

CHICKEN STEW

Notes, taken by Hope, in 1993, from social services files:
Report on Mrs Daniels (Mum), dated spring 1982:
- — We Moved into Hamilton Street – mid to end 1980.
- — Three-bedroom terraced house – very poor state of repair
- — Social Worker – wrote to the Environmental Health Officer as SW concerned. Asked them to visit us.

Don't remember them doing that.

- — Phillip is working – he pays Mum and Dad £15 a week.
- — M&D pay: £1.20 weekly off rent arrears. Fuel debts – also taken from their social security allowance.
- — They get £36.15 plus £15.75 child benefit a week. The financial situation is very low.

Three adults, three kids in that house. Financial Situation very low – No shit, Sherlock.

Mum's cooking, 1982

As I open the door, the smell of chicken stew takes over my nostrils. My house smells like my friends' houses. I am confused – tonight our house does not smell of alcohol and cigarettes. I don't want to be noticed or disturb what I am sure is my mind playing tricks on me, but I decide to investigate. Tentatively I step sideways along the corridor, back against the wall, like a climber I saw on the telly, passing along a precipice with a 100-foot drop. I shuffle forward, my small frame and hands splayed against the wall to steady my silent approach towards the kitchen and her secrets. After each step I raise my nose and fill my nostrils, checking the air. Is the yummy smell still present? I hope the aroma will stay at least until I reach the kitchen. My hunger increases with every step, every sniff of the air. New smells.

I trip. I catch the banister. I stop. I look. I listen. The person in the kitchen has not heard me, so I move on. The excitement, the possibility of a hot meal, makes me careless.

I will be in such trouble if I get caught creeping through the house. What if my tummy rumbles before I reach my viewing place?

I nearly give myself away a second time when, so keen am I to confirm we will be eating this evening, I forget to count the floorboards. I nearly stand on the fifteenth floorboard. This is the special floorboard that creaks loudly when Mum stands on it deliberately, just before coming upstairs with her friends. It's her way of telling us kids that, if we aren't already sleeping, we have to straight away pretend we are sleep. We disappear, so her friend, or an uncle, can accompany her. Just in time, I remember the floorboard. My heart races and I imagine I'm stepping over a big, life-threatening unstable crevasse on the mountain. My goal is in reach, and I grab the frame of the door, pulling myself forward with a sideways stretch step, to the final resting point. I am successful in my adventure from front door to the kitchen doorframe.

I've reached the top of the mountain.

YES!

Before looking round the doorframe, I listen to my heartbeat slowing, and as I have so often before, I hide in the corner ready to watch what's going on in the kitchen.

I bend forward to peek round the kitchen door, the frame covering half my face. With one eye I can see the kitchen, and with my bum still against the corridor wall so I don't fall, I stand there for a moment trying to control my balance and my fast breathing. This time the kitchen seems different.

I jump back, my whole frame now flat against the wall.

My mother's at the cooker!

Curiosity overtakes me. I lean forward ever so slightly more than last time. Now my whole head pops out beyond the doorframe. I want to make sure with both my eyes that my one-eye peek was not deceiving me.

Bloody hell!

I retreat and suppress a giggle. There I stand working through what I've just seen to back up the smell. My mother, the late evening sun playing with the highlights in her hair, is cooking.

I steal another peak. I giggle, silently.

She is cooking! Wait until I tell my brothers. It's not even Monday, and we have food.

I lean forward again to double-check my vision. I am half-expecting the nice surprise to be just my imagination.

Her shoes with four-inch heels are on the floor to the left-hand side of the cooker, as if she has just stepped out of them. Her red toenails, which match her long finger-nails, are exposed. Her bare feet support thin legs, a good frame. Her bottom is adorned by a tight black leather mini-skirt, the one she always wears. Her long blonde hair is, for once, tied back in a ponytail that floats down her red silk blouse and straight back. The white stove stands to atten-tion as my mother concentrates on turning up the heat on the electric ring.

For a long time I watch, admiring her elegance and her beauty. Gliding to and fro across the kitchen, stirring the pot, occasionally swearing, and muttering to her private world.

It's the first time I have ever seen my mother alone. No longer surrounded by cackling company, wine bottles, gin, whisky, cigarettes and smoke. It's the first time I have seen her work with her hands, put them in water, risk the nail varnish. She walks back and forth in the kitchen and not once does she wobble, or have to hold on to the kitchen counter for support. Maybe it is because she is not wearing those shoes. She lights a fag as she stirs the stew, pours tea from the rarely used, chipped teapot that we got from Grandma Mary.

She's drinking tea.

My mother in this moment is gorgeous. I imagine she will drink tea from now on and we shall have dinner cooked for us every night. I imagine my home will smell like other people's homes if she keeps this up. I imagine coming home from school like this every day, like the other children do, to a hug. A warm meal. A dry bed. I imagine. I imagine.

Eventually I move out to stand in the door, staring. She feels me there. She turns, slowly, and then she smiles. The fag is still hanging from her red lips. She is beautiful.

'Ah, Hope, I didn't hear you come in. How was school?'

'Fine, Mum. What's that?'

'Chicken stew. I made it. It's ready. Will you call your brothers?'

From the street my brothers rushed in responding to my call: 'Jack, Harold. We have stew!'

Their suspense is mine to build. I stand in the hall, in front of the kitchen door. My hand outstretched.

'Stop!' I command. 'Wash your hands before tea.'

'What? Tea? Hot tea? But it's not Monday. Is there, is there enough for us all?'

I beam. I nod. Decisive.

Is there?

'Tea. Mum has cooked chicken stew, for us all.'

Their eyes grow wider. I am proud to be able to tell them. Mother is in the kitchen. Mother is cooking. I can see their dreams matching mine. This will be our new normality. This will be the first day of many.

We pause, not quite knowing what to do. Their disbelief is suddenly dispelled by excitement. In unison, we three rush upstairs. The fifteenth floorboard squeals alongside our excitement. We rush like in a school race, with each other, passing each other, clamouring to get to the bathroom. Loud, happy children. A house full of joy.

'Me first! Me first!'

All rushing to wash our hands. We all reach the bathroom at the same time, no point in waiting, delaying each other as we all three squeeze through the door. We pop out at the other side, hands outstretched towards the sink. Two small steps for children, a big leap for mankind.

'Move over, Hope. You're in the way!'

'No, I'm not. I'm the tallest, let me turn the tap on.'

Three sets of tiny hands, reaching on tiptoes to find a trickle of cold water. I show my brothers how to rub hands together, as I have been told to do at school. But, unlike at school, there is no soap on the side of the sink here. The way the three of us attempt to wash our hands, you would think we have been promised sweets for a week, and a toy.

We rush down the stairs, together. Pull out the chairs with a scrape, and sit at the table, together. The food is already on the table. This is the first time we have ever sat at the table to eat. Normally the table is piled high with bottles and glasses of drink. There are three plates, only one of which is chipped. That is my one. We look for what seems like a long time at mashed potatoes and stew. Steaming-hot stew. The smell brings such pleasure. We pick up our spoons. It's gone in three minutes, and there is a delightful second helping. We all wipe the plates with our fingers and wash them clean with our tongues.

I don't remember what my mother does as we eat, so focused am I on the food.

My father did not come home that night, but nor did the house have any other male visitors. I went to bed with a strange feeling. I'd eaten. I'd eaten well. My mother cooked. I felt a little bit sick from all the food. A nice taste of being happy.

Carpet baggers, 1982

'Quick, Hope, get the front door open!'

The sight is ridiculous. Dad is struggling down the road with a huge role of carpet balanced on his shoulder. He is almost doubled over with the weight, swinging himself from side to side, struggling under the carpet towards me. I burst out laughing.

'Come on, Hope, quit that, open the door. Quick, I've just nicked this from the second-hand shop!'

He dumps the carpet in the living room just as my mum appears.

'What's that, did you bring me owt?'

'It's a carpet, love.'

Dad's hand disappears into his pocket. A face powder and a new bright-red lipstick appear. He's done well in his stealing today, and is rewarded by a kiss from my mother, before she disappears.

'Brilliant, Dad, well done!' I am pleased as punch: we have a new carpet to sit on tonight, and every night; Mum has some new make-up and Dad didn't get caught stealing any of it. The rug fits well in the living room, and no one cares about the ridiculously loud purple pattern.

My dad is the cleverest person in the world to be able to get away with this. I wish I could steal as good as him.

6

MONDAYS

I've no specific memories of any particular Monday, but they happened all the same. In all the time we lived at home, they went to the pub for the whole of Monday. Every week. A normal Monday meant Mum and Dad went to the pub, and then Mum at some point went off to King's Cross. Well, that is what they did until they got themselves banned from all the pubs in Hackney, then after that they drank at home. I had never been to this place King's Cross, didn't want to. I knew Mum made her money there, and money meant men. I never wanted to go there.

Benefits were paid out on a Monday, at the Post Office, so it was always a big day for the whole family. The excitement that the hole in my tummy would be filled that night followed me round all day. The thought of food, especially in the holidays when there were no school meals, meant I would spend the whole day working out what we would buy that night for the three of us. Kebab rolls generally.

Every week we ordered three hot delicious doner kebab rolls and a can of juice that we shared. I would rush home from school, dropping my bag at the front door, eyes focused on the same spot – the white living-room mantelpiece. There it was – a shiny blue note. The Duke of Wellington and the Queen waiting to provide me and my brothers with food that night.

Every week, the same ritual. I would look at the note, both sides, checking it was real. I knew that money was meant to last all week, but the rest of the week we managed by shoplifting or foraging, and through the kindness of neighbours. Monday was a day of treats. Satisfied my parents hadn't scammed us, I would turn on my heels, and regardless of what I had decided during the day, in the early evening we still ended up in the kebab shop. Three doner kebab rolls and a can of juice. I told my brothers we had this so that I didn't have to cook. The real reason was so that we didn't have to wait to eat.

Every week we sat on the steps across the road from the kebab shop, or sometimes we brought it home to eat in front of the TV. We ate fast, but without dropping anything. We were delighted with ourselves. Bits of meat oozing out from under the salad we never asked for but always got. Chilli sauce tingling on our lips. We tried not to let a drop of anything, even the salad, spill out. If it did, we picked it up to avoid waste and disappointment. Wiped it off our clothes or the furniture with our fingers. The three of us, every Monday from age five, four and two through to ages nine, seven and five, crowded into the kebab shop, our noses first below counter level, and then above it as we grew taller. Salivating and drooling.

This was our routine. A routine that mirrored my parents' routine of getting paid, going to the pub after leaving the money on the mantelpiece, and arriving home the next day, when we all had to be very quiet. I don't know if they ate on Mondays as we rarely saw them on that day.

On Monday evenings, with our freedom and our guaranteed meal devoured, we played. Our imagination compensated for a lack of toys.

We made up games like Burp. For this game, after eating our hot meal, we lay on the floor, hands on our tummies, and had a competition over the loudest burp. We went exploring to my brother Phillip's room. Before he left home, Phillip worked mending slot machines. He had a Space Invaders machine in his room, and he rigged it so it didn't need money. We had watched as he showed us the little men being zapped.

His room was the magic room. We were not meant to go in there without him, but we did. We marvelled at how he had decorated the ceiling and walls of his room with a real live circus tent. How he slept with his mattress under it in the middle of the floor, like the Bedouin he said. We did not know what he meant, but our imaginations loved that room. We held circus shows and Phillip swung us around in turn, holding our arms as we pretended we were trapeze artists. We liked it better when Phillip lived with us. We ate more often then. He used to get us ready for school.

Dad left him behind when we first moved into Hamilton Street. Phillip only stayed there sometimes. He was always out staying with a friend. We kids were not allowed to ask where he had gone, or when he was coming home. He left everything in his room, and because he told us we were not allowed in it, we knew he must be coming home at some point. Whenever he was gone, Phillip told me that I was the eldest at home now and I had to do my best. Each time after he left, I sat in his room, looking down the road, waiting for him to come back. Feeling he didn't like us. Trying to work out what I had done to make him leave. I didn't understand why he left.

After Dad left him behind when we moved into Princess Lodge, it took him a week to find us. But when we moved into this house, he moved in and he made his room into a circus room. He played with us. He got us up in the mornings. Phillip worked in a real job. Phillip left. I thought he left because he didn't like me. It was something I had done. After he left, looking after Jack and Harold fell to me. He only came back now and then, often on Mondays when he would buy nice things and make sure we ate proper. Sometimes he stayed over, sometimes he didn't. But he stayed less and less, and I had to do more and more. The house got more messy and Mum more angry. I did my best without Phillip. Every Monday I looked for him, but the times he came home became fewer and fewer, then seemed like not at all. All I found was the £5 waiting faithfully every week to give us some respite. We ate like adults and we laughed like children on Mondays.

Post Office, 1982

Things are chaos at home. There is less food than there ever was and it's not the time of year for rhubarb, though we still check most days. Mum and Dad have no money, so they stay home and wait for men in suits to bring them alcohol and fags. They have pissed off all the neighbours, so they don't give us brown bread jam sandwiches any more.

It's the school holidays so we don't eat every day. Neither Jack nor I feel like running around any more. Our tummies hurt, and I don't know when we are going to eat again.

We sit on the steps staring into space. Not really doing anything. Not allowed to go inside as Mum says, they 'are entertaining'.

Why can't Mum and Dad entertain us?

They are all in the kitchen and we sit outside on the steps.

I jump up and startle Jack. 'Come on, I have an idea.'

I drag Jack along the road, down the lane at the side of our house, where Mum and Dad have got mugged a couple of times. At the end of the alley, we stop, looking and listening out for the man in the long black leather coat who scares us. He even scares Mum and Dad. He isn't here, so I run out of the alley, dragging Jack behind me into the Post Office.

We queue at the sweet counter. I jump from side to side, foot to foot, like I want to wet myself. I don't really, I'm just crappin' it a bit about what we are going to do. Well, I am going 'to do', and Jack is going to enjoy.

We get near the front. It's us next. We are here, it's our turn! I take a deep breath and start explaining:

'Dad's sent us for sweets. He says you can take the money off Monday's money.'

My eyes are wide. I know my grin is cute, 'cos I practise it when I'm really bored. I shove Jack behind me as he realises what I've dragged him into.

'Are you sure?'

'Yes, Miss, promise, Miss.'

My head is nodding up and down, just like one of the Christmas donkeys whose neck moves on a spring. My smile is sincere. Jack is poking me in the back with a finger. I shove him further behind me.

'OK, how much did your dad say?'

Oh help.

'Um, he didn't really, Miss, he just said, "Get out of my face and go and get some sweets on tick."'

Jack nudges me again and I push him back.

'That sounds like your father.' A disapproving look. A look to her husband behind the other counter. He nods.

'All right, you two, a can of juice and 10p worth of chews.'

'Awww, I'm sure he'd let us have more, Miss.'

'OK, 15p each, no more.'

We both go over to the half-penny chew sweets, Mojos, my favourites, and count our 30 each, before we say, 'Thank you.'

I complete a calculation in my head.

'Can we get for Harold too, Miss? Dad said it's OK.'

'On you go then,' comes the reply.

Excited, we choose 30 more sweets and another drink.

For three weeks we do this, three weeks we get away with it. On the fourth week, Dad questions his dole money. The Post Office explains why it is short. On the fourth week, Dad comes home with a look of thunder.

'You should all be ashamed of yaselves. You shouldn't steal from family. Who taught ya to steal from family? You should know better. This money is all we've got, you bunch of thieves.'

It makes me really sad when Dad is angry with us. It makes my tummy feel funny, then I feel angry.

I shouldn't have to nick the money, should I?

7

JESUS ON THE WALL

Pretending to sleep, 1982

I'm tired as it's a school night. I've been woken up by a noise coming from the big bed. My bed is a mattress at the bottom of Mum and Dad's bed. It is, according to my father, a special place to sleep. It's a bit damp as I wet it the night before, but cannot tell anyone this. I'm a big girl and shouldn't be wetting the bed, and if they find out it's a clip round the ear for me. Besides, Mum says it's difficult to have time to wash the sheets in the bath, and then get them dry in the yard. I love playing in the yard, but hate the outside toilet. It's full of big spiders and their webs get in my face when I open the door after the spider has been busy.

Sometimes my brothers shut me in there as a game, and I get really angry with them. We used to play another game, where we would jump over the wall, blood pumping so hard we could hear it, and collect up the lemonade bottles to return them for a deposit. It was exciting and gave us some cash for food. But since the neighbours put broken glass on the walls, we can't climb over next door, so my brothers get their kicks with me instead by locking me in the toilet. I hate it.

In the bedroom I share with Mum and Dad, we have wooden floorboards, and a wardrobe I am still not allowed to go into. A mirror, where Mum does her make-up standing up. It has a little chip in the corner from I don't know when, but the day it happened Mum and Dad started shouting at each other. I watch her put on her make-up, standing there, telling me she should have a proper dresser to sit down at, with glass bottles of perfume, and powder puffs, like a proper lady. She lets me watch and listen, but all the while I wait for the time she has had enough of me. I know it's time to go when she looks at herself in the mirror for a moment, her shoulders sag a little, straighten again and 'Fuck off and play, Hope' is spat all over the mirror. The curtains flap from the draught in the window and the walls haven't been painted since we moved in. We sometimes play firemen and the smoke and water damage that happened before we moved in provide for good effects. Underneath the grime you can just see there are pretty patterns on the wallpaper. You can see how the house used to be, with a yellow and brown pattern of big daisies in a summer field. The council should come and clean it up, but I heard Dad telling Mum they haven't paid the rent, so she'd better earn it. I hope Mum gets a good job. Then I won't have to share my room with Mum and Dad and the cross of Jesus.

The cross on the wall with Jesus sacrificing himself for us scares me every time I come into this room. Jesus lives on his cross above the bed and, according to Grandma, we should always remember Jesus. I remember Jesus when I go to bed. He stares at me as I move around the room.

He's there seeing the same thing I see. I see it from my bed, which is at the bottom of Mum and Dad's bed. Jesus sees what's going on from his cross on the wall. Jesus sees the man's head and body going up and down. I see the man's bottom and legs going up and down. It's not my father. The legs and bottom are too big. He doesn't smell like my father. His trousers are at his ankles. My mother is underneath the man. She is quiet. That's not like my mum. Her head is turned towards the wall, away from me. Away from Jesus. The man is moving backwards and forwards and up and down all at the same time. Jesus must be impressed. The man is making a funny noise, like a lion on the telly. Up down. The noise matches the up and down. I know I shouldn't be watching, but it's hard not to listen. I lie back down and cover my ears. My pillow is too thin to block out his shorter rhythmic 'uh uh uh'. I screw my eyes tight, hoping they will block out the noise of this man I don't know on top of my mother. I pull my legs up tight to my chest, trying to avoid the wet patch. It's cold there. I want to rub my feet together to get rid of the cold. But I don't want them to hear me, to be caught awake. I lie still pretending to sleep, waiting for the long breath to come from the man. It will be over when I feel the bed move as the man moves from on top of my mother to lie by her side. He won't stay long. Then Dad will come to bed. Jesus watching from the wall. Me listening, lying quiet as a church mouse. Trying to stop my breathing. Keeping my breathing quieter than his so they don't know I am awake. I will be in such trouble if they know I am awake. I am meant to be sleeping. Instead I am thinking.

If Jesus could talk from his place on the wall, what would Jesus say?

A door in my face, 1982

I stare at the blue-grey door which, just a moment before, slammed shut in my face. Angry, I screamed at the man who lived behind the door,

'You smell anyway, so fuck off!'

I only went round there this time on my own 'cos the girls I normally go with have been told to stop coming. Normally we three went together. I knew he was never interested in me. When we went there he was always snapping at me, finding me annoying. So I stare at the door. Why am I surprised that when I go on my own, he shuts it in my face?

He used to serve us faggots for tea – boiled for hours, but when you're hungry you eat anything. We three girls, all from similar backgrounds, mainly went to the orange-and-brown-decorated flat on the fifth floor of the high-rise estate when we were starving and our tummies rumbled like a thunderstorm. It seems we were always starving by the end of each week.

Even though he wasn't overly nice to me, he was very nice to the other girls, so when they were there he put up with me. You would think he'd be a bit nicer to me now the others have stopped coming – he always said he liked the company, just obviously not mine.

As I was so hungry this morning, I knocked on the door

myself, put on my best smile. He opened it and shut it again, and in the middle of all that opening and shutting he asked:

'Are you on your own?'

'Yes.'

Remember to smile sweetly.

Slam! The door hit the frame so hard the walls shook.

Bastard. How am I meant to get by if you won't feed me? No one wants me. No one.

I am now standing in the outside corridor staring at the door. The other two were told by their dad to stop coming here. Their dad didn't give no reason, just said: 'Don't fuckin' go there again.' They said it's the only time their dad cared, so they did it, even though they don't know why and it is harder now for them to find food. Like me, these girls also have to look after themselves 'cos their mum and dad drink the benefits money too. I met them on a Thursday when the money had run out, and they were out looking for fag ends for their dad. They took me to their house to give their dad the findings and it was a right mess, seriously filthy. The house stank.

There's always someone worse off.

We three sat at the top of the steps outside their house, fag ends delivered. As the light faded, we discussed how hungry we were and the different ways we found food. I was careful, though, not to tell them everything, as in a way we're in competition, but I told them about which shops were easy to get food from without money. They told me how when they were really hungry they went to this old man's house and I could come too, if I liked. I liked, so I did. The first time I went, I felt so full after leaving that on the way home I persuaded them we should go once a week, and we did, for months.

Well, we went until they were told to stop going, and then he shut the door in my face. I never went there again, except to ring the doorbell and run away before he answered. My own private game of knock down ginger. Playing this didn't make me any less hungry but it made me feel a bit more in control.

A treat, 1982

We are running, creating the wind in our hair. On our way to Abney Park Cemetery to play and hunt for rhubarb. We've left the door on the latch. Mum and Dad have gone out, and won't be back today. Everything is normal. I stop short.

There's one.

Out of the corner of my eye, I see it, a can of Fanta, left in a telephone box. Every time I see one I'm really happy 'cos someone left it there for us.

As I pull open the heavy red door of the phone box, Jack and Harold stand waiting for their share. I always share. I reach up, grinning at the boys. Jack is squealing and jumping in excitement.

'Me first! Me first!'

'Jack, stop jumping up. You will hurt yourself. No, it's my turn to be first.'

And it was my turn. I shake the already opened can to see how much there is to go around. It's almost full. Someone must have opened it and forgotten about it. I grin at the expectant faces, a real treat. I take a big slug.

Immediately it hits my tongue, I spit and spray the liquid everywhere. I drop the can.

Spit, spit spit. Rubbing my mouth.

'Shite. UUUGGGG.'

Harold picks up the can and bursts out laughing, starts chanting:

'That's piss! That's piss!'

And it was.

Visiting Grandma Mary, 1983

My grandma is a short, stumpy woman who lives on her own at the top of a high-rise. Every time we come, which isn't often, she wears the same flowery pinny with pockets in the front. I don't think she keeps anything except her hands in those pockets. We are at her house now. It is a perfect house: it could be in a magazine. Her hair is perfect.

I knew we were visiting her today, 'cos Mum has been in a worse mood than normal since yesterday, and we got up to go on the bus to Kennington this morning. I like that bus. We cross the river and then go through Elephant and Castle and the big roundabouts where all the cars dodge each other. When we are on our own, we sneak into the swimming baths at the Elephant and Castle. But not when Mum is here as she is too big to slip in past the barriers unnoticed, and definitely not when we are on our way to Grandma's house. A trip here is a whole day's outing on its own. Mum always has to go home after a visit to Grandma's, as that woman wears her out, she swears she does. We can't go swimming, as Mum has to rest after a day like today. We get home, she rests in the kitchen and she gets me to pour her a drink, just how she likes it.

I am not allowed to touch anything inside Grandma's house, so me and Harold are out on the landing, looking over the balcony. It's quite high up, near the top of the block but with two floors above us. From here we can see the market below.

I love going to that market. There are rings, and shiny new and not-so-new things. Grandma buys us towels from there, but never the dress rings I so desperately want:

'They're cheap, Hope, they'll turn your fingers green.'

'Please, Mum, please, please can I have one? I want a dress ring.'

'No, Hope, want doesn't get.'

'Listen to your mum, Hope, they are cheap rubbish. Stop going on.'

My grandma moans a lot, mumbles under her breath as well as out loud. Her face seems hard, like it's never smiled. Her mouth is set in a permanent straight line, like a ruler, and when it opens it says some things in her thick London accent that make me feel creepy-crawly:

'This place isn't what it used to be, all these blacks movin' in . . . God, the smells, can't they cook British food? Why all these spices in cooking, can't see the point really . . . Coming over here, taking jobs off the likes of us, changing everything . . . I don't know, it's not right . . .'

Instead of listening, I disappear out onto the landing, and hoist myself up so I can see over the wall and breathe in the smells of the city. I love the aromas coming from the kitchen windows, the thought of families gathered together to eat. To eat, to eat, to eat. Food of different colours and smells, the noise of a pan after it has been used, clinking into the stainless steel sink, a sound of homely pleasures.

The people in the market below and the views across the rooftops are my escape into another world.

Mum and Grandma discuss things in the kitchen in low voices. Grandma always hands Mum something she can carry home on the bus, some towels, or something else for the house, when we all know Mum only came here for money.

My mother's head pops round the door.

'Hope and Harold, get back in here, now. Go sit in the living room.'

It stinks in here.

Bored, I run my finger around. There is no dust. There is a pattern of white circles on the glass table, and a tin that has a picture of Diana and Charles, who got married almost two years ago. She's wearing a blue dress and has a ring on her finger bigger than any sweet I've ever seen. I imagine their perfect life, with no fights, and wonder if their grandma gives them hugs, like mine doesn't. Even though I am not allowed, I open the tin, and steal two sweets. I pop one in my mouth and save the other for later. I stick my tongue out at the door, just as Mum comes in and tells me:

'Come on, we're off.'

I smile. I don't like coming here. I don't think my mum likes coming here. It stresses her out, and there is no drink, only tea. The last time I was here I was almost eight, but now I am nearly nine. Apart from when she came when we first moved into the house we are in now, Grandma never visits. Would probably complain about coming to see us too.

I can't remember her real name, can't remember saying, 'Cheerio.' I don't remember being told anything about my granddad, except that he's dead. I can't remember visiting or seeing her again until many years later. My grandma was never more than a stranger to me.

Birthday party, 1983

I know! I can give her one of my dolls. Which one? Which one?

My excitement at being invited by a girl at school to her birthday party means I am literally bouncing around the bedroom. Mum and Dad are out, and so far I have managed to keep my going to the girl's party a secret. She is black, and because of this, I know Mum will stop me if she finds out. The girl is nice; she speaks to me at school. I know that my parents would have a fit. When I got the invitation, all pretty, stating the time and place in the girl's handwriting, with a drawing of balloons and cake in the top right-hand corner, I knew I had to be there. I also had a chat with myself about how to make sure I got there. *I have to keep this secret and I have to find a birthday present to give her from my own toys.*

I am in the bedroom, scrabbling through my toys. I pull them all out, and place them one by one in a straight row. They stare back at me, each with its own personality, none of them jumping out at me, saying, 'Pick me.' I examine each one, turning it upside down, brushing each doll's hair down with my hands, as I do my own hair every morning. I place them back, looking at them all and decide on this one.

My route from my house to hers is all worked out. I set off, holding my present carefully in both hands.

In planning my journey, I forgot that it would take me past the skinheads who hand out leaflets telling the black people to go home.

I don't understand. They live in London, so aren't they already at home?

Even though I pass them most days, seeing them today of all days is a surprise. I cross the road, away from their ripped T-shirts and chains, tattoos and big black Doc Martens, to avoid getting one of their leaflets thrust in my hands.

I'm off to the party of a girl who just so happens to be black. So what? In my head I am brave. I imagine sticking my tongue out at the people across the road. I imagine that they see this and go home, stop handing out leaflets that mean my mum wouldn't let me go to this party, if she knew.

There are balloons on the door, so this must be the house. After I knock, the door opens and I peek round at the adult who is staring at my present and me. Inside, the food smells are delicious, and I grin. The music makes me feel even more excited and happy, more than I ever have been, except when I got my pink bike. The music is the same music as my old neighbours played, Lovers Rock. I love that music and move my shoulders to it. The children play, and I am asked to join in. I scream and laugh with them. I am so excited I want to pee, but I don't want to leave to go to the toilet just yet, in case they all disappear before I get back. I'm having too much fun.

There is food, too. I stare at the chicken; yellow things that look funny, with all squares on them; coleslaw like you see in Kentucky Fried Chicken; and my favourite, rice and peas. The peas ain't green peas like the advert on the telly: they are big red ones but I don't care, I love it all! But I wonder why no one is eating. I'm starving, and wanna eat the lot, now. We are playing in a room away from the food and I'm a little bit worried that the food will all disappear before I get to eat some, so I keep having a sneaky check by making sure I do musical statues on a spot where I can see the table through the door. At last we're all allowed into the other room and choose our plates. I fill mine up with flavours and colours that will soon fill my mouth and my eyes. I find out the yellow stuff is called corn: it tingles in my mouth, all sweet but a bit sharp at the same time. The butter melting on it makes it all soft on the outside. Mmm, it's perfect.

In the food room there are presents stacked up in a pile, all wrapped in pretty paper. While I eat I examine them. I have never seen a wrapped present before! The party girl opens them after lunch.

Ohhs and ahhs, and 'That's lovely, say thank you,' as each one is opened. 'Wow! Look at all this!'

No, no, don't throw the paper away.

It is all I can do, not to follow the paper out and rescue it from the bin. The birthday girl greets my present – a doll that fits over one of those posh toilet rolls, not the ripped-up-newspaper kind that we have, but a proper toilet roll – with the same politeness as all the other, brand-new presents. A clever adult asks:

'Has the present been used before, dear?'

I don't reply, but I know they know it has. My face goes whoosh red, matching the brightly coloured paper that is being thrown in the bin. In the bin! I can do nothing but watch as it is thrown away.

Don't throw it out, oh no don't crumple it up. No, no, give me the paper, it's a waste, it's so pretty.

8

FAMILY SECRETS

The wardrobe, 1983

I'm not allowed in the wardrobe, I know I'm not. But I'm mad at everyone today, and a little confused. I heard Mum and Dad talking last night. Mum had on her posh London voice, the one she uses sometimes when she's drunk. I think she sounds stupid. Her nails were as perfect as ever, but as there was no money to go out, they got their friend, the one who comes here quite often on Wednesdays, to bring a bottle of whisky.

I was sitting in the hall, against the wall. As usual Mum's face was not happy. After the man left, I sat on the floor-boards outside the kitchen and listened to them finishing off the whisky. The door was almost closed, but I could tell that her voice was sadder than normal.

'Do you remember Josie?'

'Of course, how could I not?'

'I can't believe I gave her up, and Susie . . . We would've managed.'

My dad did not reply to this.

Who's Susie? Who's Josie? Are they real? What do they mean, give them up? Give who up?

The voices were deeper now, quieter, not happy. I thought my mother was crying. I heard my dad's chair scrape on the floor. He must have been moving over towards her.

'Fuck off!' she screamed. Her chair scraped back now; I heard her stand and stumble. I couldn't see my dad, but imagined he backed off and sat down again. A mumbled apology:

'I'm sorry, I'm sorry. It would have been good to have a sister for Hope, but we couldn't do it, you know we couldn't. Not then. It's bad enough now. You didn't have a choice. You know that. We can't manage now. Look what you have to do to survive in this fuckin' country. Margaret fuckin' Thatcher has a lot to answer for. You were doing what you had to do. You didn't have a chance with Susie, with that old witch of a mother.'

It was the longest statement I'd ever heard my dad make. It was met with a smashing of glass and my mum's fury.

'Fuckin' hell, is that all you can think about? I had to give up my daughters and all you can think about is your fuckin' country?'

Sisters!

I didn't want them to know I knew, so I snuck backwards. She sounded really mad and the fight was turning bad. Covering my ears, I retreated to my room to avoid the crossfire.

I tried to go to sleep but the thoughts raced through my head while the screaming from downstairs wouldn't shut up. I placed my pillow over my head to try to block out the noise of my parents and the swearing that cements their relationship, bringing them closer together so they can have the joy of making up, or so my dad says. That didn't shut up my head, though.

Who is Josie? Who is Susie? Do I have a sister, sisters? Is that what Mum was saying, two sisters? One sister? Any sister? Wow! Wow! Wow! Cool. Brilliant.

Where are they? Give them up? Is that what she said, she had to give them up? She gave up the girls, so why did she keep me? Is that why she looks at me funny and sometimes calls me Josie? Mum, Mum, Mum. Where are they? Who are they?

The thoughts consumed me and knowing there's a possibility that I was not alone comforted me. I wanted to know more. I dreamed that night that the forbidden wardrobe was standing over me, calling to me. In my dream, I open the doors of the wardrobe, and the girls are in there, waiting. They're my sisters, my family. They step into the room and everything is OK again. My mum smiles all the time and no men come to the house. There are flowers on the window ledge, and we all play in the garden together with the black neighbours. My sisters wash and comb my hair and I don't have nits. Maybe they'll use the shampoo from Holloway, I still have it, but I'm not sure what to do with it, as my mum has never shown me how to wash my hair with shampoo, or at all really. They wash me and get me up for school on time. They dress me in the clothes they no longer wear and we all go to school together. My bedclothes smell nice and I don't smell of pee. We eat as a family round the table, and Mum and Dad stay in, and not just when there's no money. My mother hugs me once in a while.

A dream, just a dream. But when I wake I am both fixated on the wardrobe and in a bad mood for no reason. I look at it while I dress. It's tall, dark, walnut I think Mum said. Dad got it from the skip and polished it up nice for her. One day she will have a dresser with a mirror to go with it, so she says. Mum and Dad both lie face down in the bed next to my bed, the morning light not disturbing them at all. They are entangled in each other, still fully clothed. Dad is snoring.

I leave them to sleep and go downstairs to put the telly on, but it doesn't seem to be working. The light doesn't work either, which means they've cut us off again. When Dad gets up he will fix it. So I go out the front door and sit on the steps, elbows on knees, hands on chin, and wait until my parents wake, get up and go out to the pub. My feet never stopping tapping, my mind never moving beyond:

What's in the wardrobe?

I know, I just know, the answer is in the wardrobe. I have been warned about going looking in the wardrobe, but I just have to look today. I have no patience to wait for them to wake up and go out. I go back into the house and clean the kitchen up. There is glass all over, where Mum threw it at Dad, and the smell of whisky and smoke still lingers, but today I hardly notice, as with each sweep of the brush and wipe of the table with a towel that Grandma gave us, I think of Josie and Susie.

Where are you? Who are you?

At last, Mum and Dad get up. As I watch Mum re-apply her make-up on top of yesterday's efforts, my excitement at the prospect of going into the wardrobe builds. I'm not very good at hiding it.

'Hope, what's up with you today? Stop bouncing around. Hope, fuckin' stop it, go outside the back . . . Shut up, ya useless bitch. Get out my face and take ya brothers with ya.'

I try hard to be good in the yard, but just kick around the garden while the boys dig up worms and split them in half to make two worms. It isn't warm, but it isn't cold either. Finally, Mum and Dad go out, and I know they will be gone all day.

I sit on Mum and Dad's unmade bed and stare at it. I've been warned about going into this wardrobe many a time. My parents have caught me stealing from them so many times, I guess this is where they keep the things they don't want me to steal. The excitement builds as I stare at its bulk. The sun is streaming through the holes in the curtain, making dots on the wardrobe door. The light dances like fairies. The wardrobe is huge. Even though this is my room too, I have never seen the wardrobe open. My excitement builds as I move towards it, but I can take my time, as Mum and Dad will probably be out far into the night.

The door is heavy. I pull it back. My fingernails are caked in mud and for a moment I worry that I will leave a trace of my being here, but anticipation of the treasure means the thought is gone before it's fully formed.

The inside of the wardrobe seems vast. There is Dad's suit, the one he wears when he goes to court, and Mum's second blouse. She is wearing the other one today.

Nothing else exciting seems obvious, so I open the drawer that is inside. It sticks as I pull it out, but I manage to extract it by giving it a bit of a jiggle. I am nervous. I am excited. I am peering into the drawer within the forbidden wardrobe. Inside there are two boxes. I take the black one that looks like a cash box out first and lay it on the bed. It's not locked and I open it with both hands. My eyes are fixed on the box to see as soon as possible what is inside.

Cash! All the coins are laid out, in a plastic box, with writing. It takes me a while to read what it says on the label. The date says 15 February 1971. I quickly rip open the packet, pour all the coins out and stuff them in my pocket, hiding the packaging under my mattress.

With nothing else of interest in the money box, I return it to the wardrobe. The other box is cardboard, an old shoe-box. I didn't know my mum had ever bought shoes from a shop. The market doesn't give you the box. Even so, this greyish-white box was for shoes, and has been well thumbed, with fingerprints all over it. It's dusty and one of the corners is torn and kind of flaps up. There are splashes on it, water drops splaying outwards, like snowflakes on the window, or rain before it really starts, when little drops fall in the mud with a splash. It seems like a sad-looking box, so I lift it out with care. Without disturbing the dust, I take the lid off, careful like, and place it to one side.

I stare and stare but don't understand. Inside there are two tiny wristbands and a couple of bits of folded yellow-ish paper. Both wristbands have a hospital name written on them, but with different dates. I pick them both up at the same time. I look at one and then the other. I place them down gently on the lid, then pick up and carefully unfold both the papers. I read them slowly.

Birth certificates!

They are issued for a Susie, and a Josie. Even though I've missed a lot of school, I know how to do sums. My mum was seventeen when Susie was born. She doesn't have the same last name as me, or my dad. Josie is older than me, but younger than Phillip. She has the same last name as me. My mouth falls open. I remember last night's overheard discussion. I go over it again and again in my head. I put the baby tags and birth certificates back in their box, and leave them there in their secret store. The realisation slowly dawns.

Sisters, I really do have sisters.

It must have given Mum something tangible of her lost children. To my shame, on a visit home a few years later , I took them. I realise now that those splashes on the box must have been Mum's tears. It would be many years before I asked her about my sisters, and when in a morose mood Mum would often call me Josie. Unknown to her, from the day I opened the wardrobe, I understood a little as to why and who. But I took those wristbands and held them as if they were mine, never telling my parents that I knew. I wish I hadn't, as between one of my many moves, they were lost, the only tangible evidence I held of my sisters, and my mother held of her eldest daughters.

As for those coins, I know now that they were a special set to mark Decimalisation Day, but at nine years old they were just money to me. I was unfortunately not very sophisticated in either my stealing or my disposing of the evidence. Later on that week, Mum found the evidence, and my parents were both really upset with me. Ironic. Why would I have been any different – it was they who taught me and my brothers the art of stealing, while other parents teach their children to play, wash their hands and to read and write.

Despite my sisters being taken, or given, away, I have no recollection of Social Services ever visiting us. Rather, I recall my parents consciously emptying the gas meter because they knew that Social Services would provide money for us. We were often left at the end of the street while my parents went to the offices to demand money for the family. This money was often spent on alcohol, not us. As our neglect increased, so did the lies my parents told to Social Services, and the police. My parents did what they could to avoid having social workers visit our home, and they told us to go out when they knew someone was coming. As a result, we were rarely seen in the home, and we were not taken into care by Social Services. I wonder what, if anything, would have been different if we had been taken in earlier.

My birthday party, 1983

'Dad, can I have some party invitations?'

'What for?'

'A party, my birthday party, Dad, pleeeasssse, Dad. They have some in the Post Office.'

'OK, Hope.'

A few days later, there's still no sign of the invitations.

'Dad, have you got them yet, Dad?'

'Got what, Hope?'

'The invitations, Dad, for my party. Remember, Dad?'

'Oh right, um, yes, um, yeah, did we agree that, right, yeah? Will get them when I go to get me benefits today, that OK?'

I run to hug him. I feel myself being picked up, swung around the room, laughing. Placed down so my feet are on top of Dad's feet, and we dance. He is making the music and I am dancing on my dad's feet. The prospect of my very own party hanging in the air.

I am impatient to get home. This is a word I learnt today from my teacher.

'Hope, stop being impatient.' Then she explained what it meant.

I know the house will be empty when I get home. It's Monday, the day Mum and Dad collect their money; leave a fiver on the mantelpiece for us. Go out together; come home, separately, and alone.

I am thinking a lot about the invitations. I plan to fill them in tonight, and know exactly who I am going to invite. Six girl friends: Gemma, Emma, Lucy, Jenny, Dot and Mandy. Luckily school is at the other end of our street, so it only takes me two minutes to run home and push the door open, which as usual is left on the latch. Still running, I push the lounge door open. It still bounces against the wall, removing a little more plaster. I don't, as I normally do, check the damage. Instead I'm looking expectantly at the mantelpiece, where the fiver and the invitations should be.

There's the fiver! Where are the invitations?

I can't see them. I cross the room, check behind the fiver, but they are not there either. I search the floor in case they have fallen off. I pull the cushions off the sofa but all I find is a newspaper from the National Front stuffed down the side. I look everywhere in that room, tears once again welling and escaping. I sink with my disappointment to the floor. I cry hard, until my brothers come home. Feeling like

I've been split in two, I give them the money to go to the kebab shop. But they look at me with a big sigh. I stand up and take Jack's tiny hand, because even though my heart is broken, my tears are fresh and my eyes swollen, I cannot let them down, or let them go to the shops on their own.

I'm tapping the desk with my pencil. I love school, but still I cannot wait to get home to see my dad to ask him what happened. When I woke up this morning I decided to have the party anyway. So what if I have no invitations? I have a mouth and I can whisper to them all about the party. They all know where I live, at the end of the street.

When I get home, Dad is still in bed. I nudge him in the side, and he raises his head slightly, breath bad from booze and fags. His eyes are bloodshot, and I know he is still recovering. Normally on Tuesdays we have to be very quiet. But this is important, and my distress has turned me determined. Another word I have learnt at school. I asked the teacher what it means when you really, really want something and don't stop and you work hard to get it. Focused and determined, she said. So that is what I am being towards Dad.

I stand, fixed face, looking down at him.

'Dad, there were no invitations. What happened, Dad?'

'Well, um, well they didn't have any . . .'

I know that is a lie, 'cos I checked the Post Office yesterday morning, but I don't challenge him.

'But, Dad, did you try another shop? Dad?'

I shake him. He sits up now, rubbing his head, his eyes.

'Sorry, Hope, really I couldn't find any. I did try, I did.'

He ruffles my hair, gives me a smile. He's lost another tooth.

'Look, look, grab me jacket . . . That's a girl, 'ere 'ave this instead.'

A bright red lipstick is presented to me. I know he stole this for my mum. He steals something every day for her. A magazine, eye shadow, mascara, a lipstick.

'No, it's OK, Dad, you got that for Mum. You give it to her. It's for her. You need to get me chocolate, crisps and biscuits. My party is on the Saturday. Get them, Dad. OK, Dad.'

'Chip off the ol' block you. OK, Hope.'

It's the day of my party. I am so excited, and it's sunny. It's not my actual birthday, but the day after. On my actual birthday, it was raining. I sat the whole day, playing with a dog that a man brought. I played in the garden with the dog and a stick, as Mum entertained him upstairs. I didn't like the dog and the dog didn't like me. It won the hating stakes, though, as when I grabbed the stick one time, the dog bit me.

Mum stopped entertaining the man, and they both came running downstairs with their tops hanging out.

The man paid for the taxi to the hospital. The receptionist had a funny singing accent that the man said was Irish. 'Happy birthday, what a t'ing to happen today, of all days.'

The man said to her she had a nice Irish accent, and was it really my birthday?

'Yeah.'

He looked funny at my mum. Both of them were dressed by now. My mum had a gob on, really grumpy, but for once was quiet. I spent my birthday being angry, thoughts raced through my head, unable to let them out of my mouth.

What's he doin' here, why did he come? It was his bloody dog. He's been doing dirty things wi' my mum.

The pressure built. Finally, I was right in his face, face to face, there in the hospital waiting room.

'You're a cunt.'

There, I said it. The one word that summed up how I felt. The chant in my head began: 'Die, you dirty old man. Die, you dirty old man.'

Mum laughed, pulled the man away from me. I got an injection, and the man took us to McDonald's. First time I'd been there.

'It's American,' my mum said, her voice still all trying to be posh even though the man had given her what she wanted already – money.

I had no idea where Dad was, or what American was. I had a cheeseburger for my birthday tea, paid for by the dirty man, whose dog bit me and I called a cunt, while the doctor stood behind me with a big needle.

But today, my party day, it is really sunny and I am watching as Dad is delivering on his promise. The only problem is that, part of the deal, in my head, was that Mum and Dad weren't to be there at my party. When I thought of my party, I never imagined them being here. But they are. Both of them are sitting having a drink and Dad puts Elvis on the record player.

Oh no, don't do this. Go out, go out, go out.

Looking at the table, all laid with sandwiches and sausage rolls, sausages on a stick – but actually there is no stick, so it's just a sausage. Crisps and fizzy juice were brought out last, and having a glass of Fanta in my hand is making me forget my worry. I dance on Dad's toes and laugh as I wait for my friends to arrive.

Half an hour later, Mum and Dad are drinking together, Elvis is bringing the tone down, and I've rearranged the plates, in between looking down the street to see where they are. Two o'clock on Saturday I had said. It's now half past three.

Maybe the clock is wrong. The time is moving but the clock must be wrong.

My anxiety builds. I pace up and down, ignoring Dad's calls to 'sit at peace'. I wait, and wait and wait. Still no one comes.

My dad's watch moves on half an hour and the whisky on the table shrinks another inch.

Still no one comes.

I pace the floor, then the street. In a flash of determination, I grab my bike from the hallway and race down the street. No one is in at Lucy's house. Maggie's – try Maggie.

Maggie doesn't open the door, but speaks to me through the letterbox.

'I'm sorry, Hope, my dad won't let me come to yer house.'

I frowned. The question in my head, is 'Why?' But I don't – can't – say anything. She must know what I am thinking, because she replies anyway.

'I'm sorry, I can't.'

'Please, please come, I have crisps and juice and everything.'

'I can't. I can't. My dad won't let me. None of the girls are allowed. No one is coming to the party, Hope.'

Then she's gone with a snap of the letterbox.

I stand staring at the metal plate for a moment. I am very confused.

Dad will explain, tell me why my friends are so horrid. I will never, ever, ever, speak to them again.

I ride home. Ringing in my ears: 'No one is coming to the party.' From the street, it sounds like the party has started already. Elvis is blaring from the record player. I open the door, but the house is empty, as is the bottle of whisky left on the table. Mum and Dad have helped themselves to a snack from the party table and, although there is no note, I know that they have gone to the pub. I switch Elvis off, scratching the needle across the record, hoping never to hear it again. I listen to the silence, looking at the table full of food. I feel sick, needing to be away from here. I turn round, slam the lounge door as hard as I can, pick up my bike and go out to find someone else to play with. I vow not to ever tell anyone else that it is my birthday, ever again.

9

THE NIGHT BEFORE, THE MORNING AFTER

An evening in August, 1983

We are watching the telly. Harold, Jack and me are left in the house on our own. Sometimes sitting, sometimes joining in, pretending not to be scared. This is our favourite, *Hammer House of Horror*. There are thirteen episodes to watch, and the one that's on tonight is called 'Rude Awakening'.

It's on ITV, so during the breaks we play: I am pretending to be Eleanor Summerfield as Lady Strudwick, and Jack plays Norman Shenley, the estate agent who has nightmares and has to go to hospital. Harold is Mr Rayburn: he operates and wheels a still alive Norman to the fridge in the dead people's room. Our torn sofa cushions do their part and act as the operating table. We copy what has just been on the box, using the whole of the room, but are right back in our places as soon as the interval is over, transfixed.

Mum's child benefit book waits on the mantelpiece for Dad. It sits where I put it earlier, staring at the living room door, ready for Dad coming home. He will bounce off the edge of the door like a pinball machine, not even pretending to be sober, before he finds the strength to wobble forwards and sit down.

He's not back when it gets dark, so I tell the boys to get into their pyjamas. They complain they are a bit damp, and smelly, but so is my nightie. I can pull the wet patch to the side so I don't feel it when I sit down. I tell the boys to try the same with their pyjamas.

'If we sit careful, like, and don't move, then we can avoid the wet bits.'

Jack doesn't listen; instead he jumps from foot to foot, flapping his pyjama bottoms above his head, like a flag, trying to dry them off, before he gets tired and sits down.

Where's Dad? Where's Dad?

When the social worker, 'the old cunt', as my mother often calls her, came round earlier today, all I saw of her was her hand through the letterbox. She didn't even knock on the door; she just shoved the child benefit book through with a handwritten note.

I can read now, so I open the note. It might be something I have to go find my dad about. I know that it will be something to do with my mum. I sensed she was off on another court visit, after the drunken screaming and shouting between her and my dad late into last night. The letter explains in neat handwriting that, as expected, Mum is not coming home. Again and again, I read it. I decide not to go and find Dad. He'll be gutted when he finds out. When she is not here, he slopes around like the puppy we saw once in London Fields that had lost its mother.

'Mrs Daniels has gone to prison for soliciting – she got three months. As she went straight to Holloway, she gave me the child benefit book for you. Mondays, you collect the money. Come into the office if you need help with the children.'

Soliciting? What is that?

'Hope, why do you fuckin' question everything?' my mother's absent voice echoes in my ear.

But I want to know.

Whatever soliciting is, Mum will be gone for a few months. I am neither sad nor happy. All I know for sure is that things will be quieter now. No fighting, or men with suits and briefcases coming round. The two men who are brothers will be gone, along with the smell of drink in the kitchen, their hands on Mum's chest while I serve them drinks and Dad sits there, pretending he can't see it, thinking only of the money.

Not for a while will they all go upstairs, leaving Dad downstairs alone, with their smell lingering in the hallway and Dad drinking as if he is trying to forget something. There won't be any taxi drivers at the front door demanding money, threatening to call the police. The feeling of relief washes over me – just us and Dad for a bit.

The child benefit book is there, tempting me to hide it so I can cash it myself, but I worry about my dad thinking I've nicked it. I worry more about his reaction than having the money. So I leave it where it is. Dad will be home soon to tell us it is all OK. I try to shut my head up, keep my questions for him, but still I wonder what happened.

Why has Mum gone to prison? What do we do next?

I know Dad will be back after the pubs are closed. He's always late on the night Mum goes off, always a mixture of grumpy and sad. I will look after him, though. At least we know this time where she is.

There is no food in, so we have a glass of water from the tap. The evening rumbles on as we three kids sit in our damp nightclothes, watching *Hammer House of Horror*.

We didn't even hear them before it happened. There must have been a slow build-up of noise, a rumble that came from the end of the street. Increasing in menace as it moved towards our house. The angry crowd, male and female voices, fresh from the pub. A huge wave rounding its way along the pavement, the elements egging each other along the street. A wave of destructive thoughts following a wall of angry people. What did they think they were doing? Maybe they didn't think.

They definitely didn't think.

I hear someone scream and realise it's me. The boys sit in stunned silence. In the middle of the floor of our lounge there is a log surrounded by tiny shards and big triangular-shaped pieces of glass. The noise, sudden like a firework, bounces around the walls. Instinct sets in. I cross to the sofa, scoop my brothers up, move them along, as we all duck low. I whisper with fear and desperation.

'Come on, come on!'

Eyes darting, looking for a safe place to go.

'Oh no, oh no, oh no.' My head and body shake, but I try not to show my feelings. I push the boys out along the wall towards the hall.

'Are you hurt? Are you hurt?'

Both meet me with silence and with wide eyes full of fear. Each shakes his head. We are interrupted once again. An ambush of bricks and planks of wood, each smashing a hole in the window and bouncing across the living-room floor. A barrage of items collected from back gardens and lanes are being projected one after another, each crashing into our home, transformed from ordinary items into an unstoppable trail of missiles. We duck low, all three of us breathing heavily in unison, and we all run up the stairs together. I push the boys into the back bedroom, instructions flying along with the bricks and sticks.

'Lock the door and don't come out till I tell you.'

The sound of an angry crowd builds up outside our front door.

'Slaaag.'

'Whore.'

'Cunt.'

'Fuckin' bitch.'

Screaming adults, baying for blood.

Oh shit, they're at the front door.

Bang. Bang. Bang. On the front door.

I crouch at the top of the stairs, feral in my fear, in protecting my brothers.

Should I open the door? Tell them we are here on our own? Just me and my two young brothers?

They are hammering on it. I want to cry.

Thud. Thud. There is another crash of glass from the living room.

I run up and down the wooden stairs.

'Please leave us alone.'

Can they hear me? Mummy. I want my mummy.

Until tonight, people have either ignored us or pitied us. I didn't like it, but I could have lived with it. I run to the upstairs front room to peek out. A crowd of people, all adults, neighbours some of them. Angry. Screaming. Shouting. Baying. A tattooed arm raised back behind the head, a good throw. Someone congratulates him by nodding and clapping his shoulder.

Is that the man who gives us kids sugar sandwiches, standing at the back? Shit.

Half a brick that time, straight into the room I am in. Upstairs they aim, upstairs they hit. The windows relent with the pressure. Smash straight through. Glass scatters everywhere. I jump back. Others raise their arms.

'Please leave us alone.'

There is a pile of wood, bricks and stone, each item ready to be turned, by men and women, away from their intended purpose and thrown, as a missile of terror, into our home.

'Bitch, you been near my man.'

'Dirty whore!'

'Get out!'

The pack is taking delight in making small and large holes in the windows of our home, where I, age nine, stand in fear. Where we, the youngest three of the family, are left alone on this warm summer evening, to face this crowd. A night when even the birds stopped singing.

Why do they hate us? Mummy, did you have sex with some-one's dad? Sex is dirty. Sex is bad.

Up and down the stairs I run – wanting to do something propels me down the stairs, fear sends me back up. Up and down the stairs. Getting to the door, never opening it to tell them we are here, alone. They are fighting children. Mum has already gone. Dad will be home soon.

Daddy, Dad.

I sob the words each time I reach the bottom of the stairs. Speaking to the back of the front door, hoping the crowd outside will hear me and go.

'Leave us be, please, please go away, leave us be. Mum's not here. Go away.'

Another arm raised, and the warm August evening air follows a brick into the room, bringing with it a hint of autumn.

The windows have all gone. I back off, muttering to myself all the time, hoping they have gone. I stand at the bottom of the stairs. The crowd is quieter now.

Have they finished? Please, please have they gone?

I hold on to the broken banister. I sit. I listen. I hear a spraying sound, not sure what it is, but it is on the front door. I am unable to do anything but let my heart break – my chest rising and falling fast, my head thumping – so I give up. I sit and wait to see if it is over. Tears roll down my face and I wrap my arms around my knees, for comfort. Wait, waiting for the crowd to go home. Rocking myself backwards and forwards on the step. Waiting for them to look up at our broken home and go to their own homes.

Is that where their plans and debates and shouts of

Come on! had taken place, in their own homes? How did they come to be here? Did they check this was the right house? Did they say, 'This is the place.'?

We did not hear them, did not know they were coming for us.

We are children. They are adults. A crowd of adults had discussed this and made a choice. They were armed, as the nursery rhyme goes, with sticks and stones that break your bones.

It's quieter now, and the spraying sound has stopped. I run upstairs to the bedroom I share with my parents to see if they have really gone. The last of them are walking away now, up the road, laughing, screaming, like animals.

Slowly I creep downstairs, open the front door. The tears come thick and fast, running into my open mouth. My hands are shaking; my whole body joins in. I stare at the final act, the closing scene, the final present of these people. Red paint on our blue front door. I can read now.

'SLAG.'

Turning back indoors, I walk around the house, placing my bare feet carefully among the glass, hands at my side, head down. Alone. No one came to help us, me. Everyone round here, they all hate us kids. I can't see anything of the floor or the sofa. Everything is broken, covered in planks of wood, logs, massive shards of glass, bricks, and tiny chips of glass. There is a brick inside the telly.

Remembering my brothers, I run upstairs. Jack is crying so hard, he is choking. My heart breaks, again. We move into the hall and cry together, huddled in a bundle of wet nightclothes on the stairs, surrounded by glass and the baying crowd echoing in our ears.

'Slag!'

'Whore!'

I am still sitting there when my older brother Phillip comes home. In a daze, we walk round the house together in silence. He holds my hand.

Glass all over the floor. He watches where I put my feet.

He pulls me away as I get a brush to start clearing up. He gets some stuff for me to barricade the door and says he has to go out again. He tells my younger brothers, who are still crying and shaking, to lock themselves in the bedroom. He's going to leave me alone.

'No, Hope, I need to go out again, and you need to go to bed. Only let Dad in, when he comes home.'

Phillip runs his eyes round the living room with a look I don't understand, and leaves. I go into the living room, where the windows are open to the elements. My knees give way, I sink to the floor, the room is filled with the weight of a nine-year-old's rhythmic sobs.

I hate my life. I want it to end. When will it end?

Never have I felt so alone, so unable to cope.

I relive this moment again and again, throughout my life. The feeling of fear, of loathing, returns time after time. Flashbacks take me over, as if that evening is once again my present. It is real, all over again. Memory and feelings are set off by the sight of a bay window in a street in a town somewhere. I will live this evening time and again. It never changes. Even though I try to fight my mind going back there, it takes me back anyway. Some cruel state I can never leave, I go back to the past which feels like the present. The feelings of desperation and fear overwhelm me, just as they did then.

There I sit until my brother comes home.

'The police have said we gotta barricade the door and run round there if they come back. Help me get the sofa out.'

I am dead tired, yet I struggle with him to drag our huge, smelly old sofa out, and push it up against the door.

'I'll listen out for Dad, Hope. You go to bed.'

Even though we clear the glass from my mattress, the room is cold without a window and I can't sleep. I toss and turn, never quite avoiding the wet patch, reminding me of all the previous nights' bedwetting.

I sit up with a start, as my father is banging on the front door, unable to get past the barricade. He is drunk, screaming:

'Let me in, you bastards, you've locked me out. For fuck's sake. What the fu—?'

Bang. Bang. Bang.

I hear Phillip answer the call. I jump up, wipe my tears. *Daddy has come home.*

When I get to the top of the stairs, my father is at the bottom, swaying like a spinning top, trying to focus.

'What the fuck's happened?'

'Fuck knows, Dad. You know the poor little bastards were here on their own. Where the fuck's Mum? King's Cross? Again?'

'No, no, she's not there . . .'

My dad is more drunk than I've ever seen him. Slurring

and staggering all over the place, bumping off walls. Grinding glass into the floor.

'Let me get the fuck to bed, will ya?'

'Bed, Hope,' Phillip says, with such a sad look on his face.

I lie in bed, thinking over and over: *Why are people so nasty? What have we done? What am I going to do? I hate, hate, hate living my life.*

Tears escape once more, rolling from my face onto the damp pillow. With an angry hand, I brush them away, wipe my eyes with both hands in a big sweeping motion.

This won't beat me. This won't beat me. This won't beat me.

It soothes me, like counting sheep.

This won't beat me. This won't beat me. This won't beat me.

I drift off, but am jolted back by a crash in the toilet, and my dad screams out.

He's just fallen over, he will get up in a minute.

I turn over and drift back into a fitful night's sleep.

When I wake the next morning, I run down to the toilet. I stop short at the door.

My dad is on the floor, slumped, in a pool of runny shit. He is covered in it. I retch. More tears. I crouch down. Shake him.

'Dad, get up, Dad, ya covered in shit. Get up, will ya.'

I leave him. I run back upstairs and strip my soaking nightie off. It stinks of wee. I pull on the same dirty clothes. *They smell*, I think, not for the first time. I head downstairs to get the broom.

I have to clear this up, have to clear it up.

I throw open the front door, so angry that I want to kill someone with the shards of glass that are covering our house. I set to work with my broom, sweeping the glass into piles.

'Hope, fucking leave it alone, will ya,' my dad screams out from upstairs. He must have woken and gone up to bed.

I run upstairs, wanting to tell my dad: 'Sort it out.'

Instead I stop short. For the second time that morning, my dad shocks me. He is sitting on the edge of the bed, sobbing. I dissolve. Uncontrollable tears from us both. I go to hug him, but don't. My big strong dad, who I love so much, is crying, pleading with no one that can help, 'Someone help me.'

I look at him, and see him properly. Something in me snaps.

I won't do this any more. My head hurts so bad. My heart feels like it's going to break.

I leave him to his tears, and go to wake the boys. I try to think of something nice to do today.

'We're going up the Elephant and Castle, swimming.'

Excited, they jump up, grab some clothes and scramble out of the house after me. We catch the bus. I play the game, letting them think everything's OK, letting them swim, thinking hard all the while.

What can I do? I can't put up with this life no more.

On the way home on the bus, we are all tired but a bit more relaxed. I look out of the window, my thoughts following me between bus stops, but still no answer comes.

What do I do? Where can we go?

I see it, Stokie Nick.

Stokie Nick!

For the first time in a while, I see a solution, feel a rush of something good rising up from my tummy.

'Off, boys, we're going in 'ere.'

We clamber off the bus and I usher them in. I'm not bothered by the nick, as I've been in here loads of times looking for either my mum or dad. I see the copper's face, and relax.

I'm safe, now. I know I am.

10

SAFE AT LAST

Stokie Nick, 18 August 1983

We are sitting in a row, Me, Harold and Jack. In the reception of Stokie Police Station. Left to right, we sit in the order we were born. My feet are tapping the metal leg of the chair. I can't help it. I do want to sit still, but I can't. My leg is moving as if I am plugged into the mains. I've been told we will get chocolate if we wait quietly, like. I want chocolate, so I am trying really hard. I want Jack and Harold to have chocolate, too.

When we came in, the copper, who I now know as Jim, leaned over the counter and peered at us.

'We ain't going home. Can't live there no more. I want to see my social worker.' He opened a big file and wrote some stuff in it, asked me if I could let him know where the hands on the clock were, so he could write down the time. 11.30. Asked me if I knew what day it was.

'Thursday.'

He smiled.

I've seen this copper in here before: he always seems to be behind the desk when I've been in to look for Mum and Dad. Is he here all the time? Does he get bored working behind that desk all day?

He is kind. I imagined what it would be like if he were my dad – something I always do when I meet a kind adult.

'All right, young lady, we will see what we can do. Sit there.' He pointed to four chairs.

There are only three of us, so I arranged Harold and Jack, leaving one space free. Thinking of Phillip. Jack won't let go of my hand. The copper got on the phone. He was on the phone for a long time. This is the third number he has dialled. I can't hear what he is saying.

Oh shit, what if he is phoning the pubs to get my dad to take us home?

The copper smiles at us each time he dials a number. I know he is very nice, and we all three now think he is even nicer as he's just given me the promised Dairy Milk chocolate and the boys some sweets.

We wait. He says we have to sit here until the social worker comes. I'm not sure how long that means, but I do know it has been a long time already and I am getting bored. He keeps smiling at us, the copper. My feet won't stop banging the side of the chair. My eyes keep moving to the door every time it opens.

Other coppers come in and stare at us, give a little smile, then move off somewhere through the door at the side of the desk. Everyone who passes through the reception from the front door into the station stops for a second and stares at us. If they put their elbow on the counter, just like Dad does at the pub, and stand there too long staring, Jim waves his hand, or covers the phone and asks: 'Waiting for a bus?'

I smile when he says this. Harold and Jack sit stock still, the whole time, saying nothing. They are leaving everything to me.

Am I doing the right thing? Dad will be really angry.

We wait and wait for a really long time. As we've had our chocolate, there is no reason to sit still. I walk about the room, looking at the posters on the wall, but as I have to pull my neck back really far to read them, I don't bother. I can see out the window and look outside for a minute – the normal world is continuing outside, with people doing their shopping. I feel like we are in a bubble. My shoulders feel heavy. I hear Jim talking about a 'Place of Safety Order'. I don't know what it is, but it has safety in the title, so that must be all right. I am scared now. I feel overwhelmed by the steps I am finally taking. This is it, we are escaping at last. I start to cry, and am unable to stop. A female copper, with a lovely pretty face, comes into the room and puts her arm round me. Immediately I have married her off with Jim, and they are both our parents, and will take us home.

'Hope, would you and your brothers like some milk?'

Milk! How lovely is this place . . . ? Why do my parents hate it here? Stokie Nick is a beautiful place.

I look at the boys, Jack with his blonde hair, Harold with brown. Both look so tiny, eyes wide with something sad. I suck my cheeks in to try and make Harold and Jack laugh. It takes me a minute, and then they do. I pat Jack's hand.

'It's going to be all right, Jack, really it is.'

Out of the corner of the window, walking down the street, I see Phillip.

Phillip!

'Phillip. Phillip.' I bang on the window, distracting Jim. He makes a motion to the pretty copper who has just come back in the door with our milk. I tell her, 'It's Phillip, my brother, get Phillip.'

She turns round and goes back outside. I stand in the doorway, wanting to run to Phillip, but also not wanting to leave the nick.

A northern female voice that is friendly for a copper says,

'Phillip, come here, mate. Hope and the boys are here.'

I suck one side of my cheek in, my lips stick out to the side. Will Phillip be angry?

As soon as he walks in the door, I throw my arms around him.

'I'm not going home, we can't live there no more, Phillip. I want us all to be in care. Jim is going to help us.' I turn to look at Jim. He nods.

Phillip is a bit clumsy but he lets me cling to him and pats my back. It's comforting. I see him look at Jim. Is Phillip scared too? Jim nods again. Phillip unwraps my hands from round his body, pushes me off him. Goes over to the counter.

'Can you really help us?'

A nod from Jim, and I want to cry. But I don't.

Chesterfields Children's Home, 18 August 1983

I feel a bit strange. I keep pulling my bottom lip inside my mouth and scraping my top teeth over it, then chewing on my top lip. The social worker came to get us from the cop shop. She filled in some more forms and now she is taking us to a place called Chesterfields. She says it's nice, but it is in Highgate, not Hackney. Phillip is being sorted out by the social worker too: she is finding him his own place to stay. A bedsit. Harold, Jack and me, we will stay together.

Phillip hugged us all, tightly in turn. Said he will come and visit us soon, like we are off to prison. We watched him go down the steps of the police station with another social worker who I've never seen before. Phillip looked younger, smaller, but his shoulders were straighter. He looked a bit like I feel.

My heart hurt, and I suddenly didn't want to go through with this any more. I didn't want Phillip to be on his own. I wanted to go home, to Dad. I started to panic.

'Phillip,' I screamed, 'come back, we'll all go home!'

I ran down the steps and grabbed his legs.

'Hope, stop it, we can't go home now, it's too late.'

I couldn't stop myself: I once again felt the tears streaming down my face. I cried, screamed, I didn't care who saw me. The pretty copper held me, rocked me, whispered in my ear, 'Hope, you are a good girl, Hope, you are a good girl,' over and over, until at last I weakened and collapsed into her arms.

I turned round to look at her face. She too had tears running down her beautiful face. *I wish, I wish, I wish she would take us all home.* I felt like bursting, I was wishing so hard. She told me: 'Go with the lady social worker, Hope. Be the brave girl we know you can be.'

She led me to where my brothers and the social worker were already standing by the car. She handed me over at the door, giving my hand directly into the social worker's hand. One hand to another. With a heavy heart, I watched her go back into the nick. I wiped my eyes, straightened myself up, and stood on my own. I was ready to go.

Dad must know by now that we're not coming home. I'm going to get into such trouble. I shouldn't have snitched on them. Daddy, Daddy, oh no, should I have done this? I have grassed, I shouldn't have grassed them up. Why did I tell? He will blame me for taking the boys away. What if the social worker tells him it was me? Poor Daddy. I love you, but I just can't live like that, Daddy. I'm sorry, Daddy, I'm sorry.

The memory of last night is suddenly back with me. I'm reliving it, like it's real. A flashback that blocks everything else out. I am reliving it. Oh no! People I recognise are standing outside our house. They're screaming about Mum, I know it's about Mum. I am sitting at the bottom of the stairs thinking the door is going to burst open and they will come in to kill us. Now it's the next morning. I'm in the house upstairs staring at Dad whose shirt is patterned with shit and sick and he is crying. I look at Dad, but can still hear the noise of the people, the smash of the windows as bricks hurl through. I am reliving both nightmares at the same time. I'm shaking. Someone is shaking me.

'Hope, Hope, are you OK? You are crying, sweetheart. Are you OK?' The car has stopped and my social worker is kneeling in front of me. Her face has little lines between her eyes above her nose. Apart from the frown, she has nice skin, not like my mum.

'Are you all right? You looked like you weren't here for a minute.'

'Yeah, course I am.'

I've done it now, I've grassed my parents up, and there's no going back.

She leads us to the bottom of a flight of steps. There is a huge blue door in front of us.

I don't know, I don't know, I don't know. Isn't there somewhere else we can go? This is a big house.

The social worker notices I'm hanging back, kicking my feet on the bottom step. Biting my lip, again. She smiles, 'Come on, Hope, don't be shy.'

My clothes aren't right, they're dirty. I don't have any other clothes, I left them all at home. How am I going to get my clothes from home? Dad just stole me two new nighties from the jumble. I love those nighties, I want them to be here too.

The door opens to a different kind of chaos. I peek my head round the social worker's skirt to see what's going on. Jack and Harold are behind me, and they have a peek, too. There are lots of people there, children and adults. Children older and younger than me.

I don't want to go in, please, Miss, please. Let us go. We can stay somewhere else. We'll be OK. I really don't want to go in now.

We are ushered in. The three of us stand together like little bunnies, very close together, touching shoulder to shoulder, and Jack is holding my hand, like he has since we left the police station. We stand and stare at the people running from room to room, and those standing putting on their shoes and coats in the hall. They take no notice of us.

'Right, you lot, everyone ready for a trip to the heath?'

There is laughter here.

It's HUGE. It feels kinda nice.

They all move past us. In a rush of colours, ages and short sentences that I think are directed at us.

'Hi.'

'Hi.' A small wave.

'See you later.' A hand is raised in greeting.

They leave, and it is quieter. A man comes towards us. Crouches down to Jack's eye level. I am looking down on him, but he looks up at me, then to each of us in turn.

'Hi, I am Craig. I'm one of the residential social workers here . . .'

A what?

He carries on, 'that's just another way of saying I'm one of the people here who, from now on will be looking after you three to make sure you are safe, fed and watered.'

He smiles, a big white-toothed grin that goes into his eyes. It makes me feel warm. He carries on:

'Would you like something to eat?'

We nod all together.

They ask if we want beans on toast, with butter. There is a room off the kitchen: it is stacked full with cans of food and boxes of cereals and juice. All stacked high like the supermarket. I am asked to go in there to get the beans. I grin. The room of food is bigger than our kitchen at home. I am told it is called a larder. You can walk in and out of it, and I do, a number of times. Into the larder, walk around.

Wow, cornflakes.

Walk back out into the kitchen. The man is making us toast. I go back into the larder.

'Biscuits!' Out into the kitchen.

'Hope, please can you find me the butter?'

Butter! Wow!

My excitement means I am in overdrive. I know this, but I don't care.

There is so much food here, a whole room you can walk into and it's full of food.

I ask a new question each time I get back into the kitchen

from the larder. I think a new question with every discovery.

What's in the kitchen cupboards if the larder is so full?

I run around the kitchen, opening and closing all the doors, looking in all the cupboards. They are all full. Each cupboard springs a new question into my mind. I ask each one and don't wait for a full answer before I ask my next question.

'Where are we? What are we doing here? What's that? How much food do you have in the cupboard? Why is it called a larder? You can walk into it, how come? How many children stay here that you have all this food? Who are the adults, is the food for them too? Do I have my own room? Where do Jack and Harold sleep? Can we eat any time we like? What we like, even cornflakes?'

All the while, a parallel set of questions is in my mind.

Is it real?

Craig tells us the beans and toast is almost ready. 'Right, kids, today we do lots for you, tomorrow we all pitch in. OK? There are twenty kids living here and everyone does their bit. Today we set the table for you, but tomorrow we ask you to help the other kids. Someone will show you how. Please can you go to the bathroom, over there, and wash your hands, kids, use the soap please. That's it, thank you.'

Wide-eyed, we do as we are told. I start to break up the bread and beans, blow on them for Jack. Pick up a piece of bread and beans to feed him.

The adults are watching us.

'Hope, let Jack feed himself.'

'But I always feed him.'

'OK.' I see Craig give the social worker a look.

'Can you use the knife and fork, or even the spoon please, Hope?'

'Wha'? Why? But we use our fingers.'

'Not here. Please can you use the fork and knife? Jack can have a spoon if that is easier.'

I pause; the boys pause. They sit on their hands and we all stare at the plates in front of us. I bite my lip. Harold bows his head, and looks at me sideways. I look up at Craig. My hand moves over my mouth in a fist. I bite my nail. I try to concentrate but my head is full to bursting. I stare at the knife and fork. My eyes fill with water and the knife and fork go blurry.

We don't use knives or forks or spoons at home. I've disappointed him already. I'm a failure.

I look up at him. He asks again, firm this time.

'Hope, use the knife and fork please.'

'How?'

Pear tree, 1983

I am sitting under the pear tree. My tummy has been full since we got here, and I am wearing my new clothes. We are allowed to pick pears from the tree, but have to wait until they are ready. When we first got here, we took some and we all got tummy ache. Craig has promised to tell me when they are ready. I hope he doesn't break this promise. I know the pears are all still a bit hard, as Jack, Harold and I got one this morning to try.

Harold is showing Jack how to play on the swing and the climbing frame. It's very good here. We have our own play park in the garden. I've found out lots of children just like us live here. I always thought we were alone.

It's nice to know that there are other kids like us who know what we been through.

I am thinking about the talk the social worker just gave me. She didn't let me speak much, and told me I had to hold on to my questions until the end. But by the time she finished I had forgotten most of them and just said, 'It is OK, I understand.' I didn't want to disappoint her, or tell her something she didn't want to hear.

We are going back to our old primary school, which is a long way away, and at the other end of the street we used to live in. Jack is in primary school too this year, so we will all go on the kids' home bus together. We will go early in the morning and it'll drop us off at the school gate. Craig will collect us in the evening and we mustn't go with anyone else. I think it's good we are all together, because I don't like it when I can't see Jack or Harold. I worry. The staff here say I am very 'anxious' and I carry around a lot of 'anxiety'. I think it's the same word. I have been saving the word up to ask my new teacher at school. It is a big word, so when I ask her she will be impressed I have heard the word, and that I need to know because I have been told that I am 'an anxious child'.

The social worker told me that Mum and Dad now know we will stay here for a while. She is applying for us to become 'Wards of Court'. I don't know what that means either, but it's OK because we all like it here. She says not to worry about it until it happens, if it happens.

What will happen if it doesn't? Do we have to go home? Oh no, I don't want to go home. Mum'll kill me.

I think of home. I think of here. The differences here are so many I cannot count them on all my fingers and toes.

The biggest one is the amount of food, and that there is heat available all the time, and no ugly old men, or drinking or adults fighting. Even if it is not on, there is heat and hot water when we want it. I check this most days, by turning on the tap, waiting for the day it stays cold. It always turns hot, and when I asked Craig about how many 50 pences are used up in the meter, Craig tells me there is no 50p meter. He tells me it's not like at home where you had to put 50ps in the meter.

Which I think Mum and Dad robbed.

The gas man came to Chesterfields this morning and he was let in with a friendly 'Hello'. I watched him read the meter and leave after having a cup of tea. At our house, the gas man was never let in to collect the money, until Mum and Dad learnt how to rig the meter.

How are Mum and Dad? I hope they're OK now we aren't there. It's my fault we aren't there. She is gonna kill me.

Here we have heat all the time, even in summer evenings, if it's a bit chilly outside. I don't really think about it now. At home we were not allowed to put the fire on when my parents weren't in. I did, though, and we made toast on it when we had bread. At home I figured they had heat in the pub and, as the meter was rigged to always show we were in credit, they wouldn't know anyhow. Here there is a toaster and there is always bread.

11

FIRST VISIT

Presents, 1983

'Your parents are coming to visit, on Sunday.'

'Shit.'

'Hope, what have we told you about swearing?'

'I know, sorry, but SHIT.'

I had not thought this through. I thought we would never see them again. Be safe.

What? Why? Shit. They will give me such a hard time. Fuck. Mum will blame me. I've told Craig all about the night before we came into care. He says it's not my fault and I did the right thing, but I'm not so sure. I took everyone into care. We shouldn't have told. Mum was always telling us not to tell, and I told. Mum will blame me. Dad will hate me.

I see them walking up the path. I run to the bathroom to check my eyes in the mirror. They are still red with crying all morning, but I still hope Mum and Dad won't notice. The cool water hits my face. If I stay here, maybe they will forget to see me. Maybe they won't want to see me. My friend Jane finds me still in the girl's communal bathroom.

'They are here, you've to come down.'

I follow her.

Dad has a bag of stuff for us. Presents.

I look at Mum. She looks furious. The boys run to Mum and Dad and give them huge hugs, like I-really-missed-you-and-don't-want-to-let-go hugs. I stand in the doorway until Craig gently guides me by the shoulders into the room. Quietly saying, just so I can hear, 'It's OK, Hope, we are here.'

I really want to see my Dad, and have been looking forward to this. I wish it was just Dad who'd come and that my mum wasn't here.

Dad has brought us a bag of presents. One each. Excited, we open them. My nighties! I pull them out. I try to mimic the tone of voice the girl at the party had when she said thanks for something she didn't really want.

'Thanks, Dad!'

They look grubby. I will hide them underneath my side table. I don't want to put them in the drawer with my new clothes.

I am looking through the bag. I hear my mother's voice. I don't need to look at her to know her gaze is as hard as the tone of her voice. Both are directed at me:

'Why did you go to Stokie Nick, Hope? Why didn't you just stay at home like we fuckin' told you to? Creating all this fuckin' mess? Givin' yer dad an' I trouble? You know wha' I mean?'

'I was scared to go home.'

'Fucking scared? You cunt. What was there to be scared about?'

'Just scared, Mum. It ain't safe for me an' the boys. Dad, tell her, it ain't safe.'

'I don't understand, Hope,' he says. 'We were getting on OK. It was a struggle, sometimes, but we looked after you kids. We did OK. We managed. You didn't need to do this, Hope, you really didn't.'

I try to change the subject. 'The kids' home tried to cut our hair, Mum. But the hairdresser turned us away 'cos our hair was full of nits.'

Before I can even think straight, or realise this is the wrong thing to say, she is up out of her chair and she is off. I don't follow her, but can hear her clumping up the stairs to the office. She is arguing with the staff. Dad doesn't move.

Harold says: 'Oops, oops . . . You really dunnit now.'

I cover my ears. That's the last time I tell her anything else that goes on here. Never, never. Oh stop it, Mum. Stop it!

I want to curl up in a little ball of embarrassment until she shuts up screaming at the staff and goes away.

Learning the rules, 1983

They aren't letting me feed Jack any more. Craig says Jack can manage himself.

'He's got to learn. You need to concentrate on looking after yourself, Hope. Learn the rules, and enjoy yourself. Go play some outside in the garden. We shall look after Jack.'

His voice is always the same level, very calm, not up and down or loud. I know he says what he means even though he doesn't shout. None of the adults here seems to shout. Still, I want to look after Jack, make sure he is OK. They don't know him like I do.

Feeding Jack, that's my job, that is what I do. Jack is mine, mine, mine. You don't know how to look after him. I do.

Jack agrees with the adults. Maybe it's because there are lots of different types of food. Stuff we have never seen on our plate before, cabbage and beans, ham and eggs! Fresh eggs! Puddings that are so sweet they melt in our mouths, and I want the flavours to stay forever. I make sure I take some of the food off every plate and put it in my pocket, for safety.

We can't be sure we shall get food later, must keep some. I have a box under my bed, that's where I keep my food. I need to get a lock on it so no one else can steal it.

Jack learns to eat like the other children eat, and soon he stops wetting the bed. I am the only one of my age who still wets the bed, but not as much as I used to.

It's less confusing here, now I know all the rules. I know what time bedtime is; what time breakfast is; what seat is ours; what we are allowed, and not allowed, to say at the table. What a dinner table is. What pocket money is, and that we get some. A clothing allowance; a key worker; what jobs we have to do around the house. My favourite job is setting the table with knives and forks and a glass each and salt and pepper. It takes me a little while to learn how to use the knife and fork rather than my fingers.

Jack no longer wants me to feed him or put him to bed. Sometimes at night, just before I fall asleep, a feeling of being all alone creeps into my bedroom. In the dark, I feel I have lost everything, and that it's all my fault.

Strawberry Shortcake, 1983

They have just done up my room. I'm so excited, I keep having to go to the toilet as I don't want to wet the bed. I haven't, even though I've been going to bed early every night this week, just to lie in bed.

I still share a room, but have a single bed of my own, not a bunk bed. The younger girls in my room are in the bunks. I have a duvet, not a blanket. But the best bit of all is that I have a Strawberry Shortcake duvet cover that wraps itself around me, so comfy and warm. There is no place I would rather be than my room with its pink carpet, pink curtains and my own bedside cabinet. They are all mine. My brothers are down the hall. We are safe and we are warm. There is more food here than I've ever seen in my life, and I am still learning what it all is. Sometimes I eat so much I am sick. Craig asks:

'Hope, are you overeating, again?'

So I smile at him and sneak some away for later. I have a box under my Strawberry Shortcake bed. I feel safe, and I have been told it is OK to grin from ear to ear when I am happy.

A meeting, 1983

We are going to have a case conference.

I wish people would explain what things are to me. It's confusing, all this stuff.

I imagine a big room of people listening to a person standing at the front, talking to everyone about suitcases. Me in the audience.

We are preparing for the case conference. I wonder if I should have brought my bag, the one Dad brought me with the nighties in. Craig says no, it's fine, we are not moving, just having a discussion. When I don't know what discussion means, he explains it means a talk, and the talk is about me, Jack and Harold. That worries me.

My social worker is sitting on one side of the room. Craig is here, and I am with my key worker, Janet. She is lovely. She is smiling at me, pleased with what the social worker is saying.

'How are you, Hope?'

'Fine, thanks.'

'We are having a case conference soon. We need to know what you want, Hope.'

'Do I go to the conference?'

Craig says, 'Maybe someone should explain to Hope what a case conference is . . .'

He says it with a question in his voice, and I am guessing who 'someone' is when my social worker speaks – it must be her:

'No, a case conference is a group of people who work on your behalf. Craig, myself and Janet attend. There is my boss, head of social work, and someone from the police.'

The police!

This freaks me out.

'The police? Why are they there? If you're all speakin' about me, why am I not there?'

She carries on: 'We all want what is best for you and your brothers, Hope.'

There is a strange look between Craig and Janet. I know I'm not meant to see it.

'We will ask you, here today, what you want. We write it down and Craig and Janet will give a report on how you are, and we all decide what to do next. This one is a very important meeting, Hope, as we are asking the court to be your guardian.'

What the fuck?

'What, like a report at school?'

'Kind of, yes.'

Have I been good enough, have I done what they asked me?

'What about Mum and Dad?' My voice is small.

Janet places a hand on my knee and holds a hand up to make sure the social worker stays quiet. Like Mum does to Dad, but different. Janet starts to speak:

'Hope, you understand your mum and dad can't cope with having all you children, right? That you've been very brave and told us what it was like for you when you lived at home? How you had to find your own food and were left on your own? How it was cold?'

Nodding, I breathe in and sit up straight to stop the tears falling from my face.

'Well, even though they cannot cope, your mum and dad still want the three of you living with them. So we need to ask a judge whether or not we can still look after you here.'

Oh crap.

'But that means we have to have a meeting about you and the boys, but you can't be there, Hope. It needs to be just adults. I promise we will tell them whatever you tell us here.'

'Why can't I say it myself? It's my life. I don't want to go home. I want to have a foster family of my own, like Lisa is having. I want one of the families who come to visit the home, to pick which kid they want, to pick me. They never choose me. I hate them all. I want to stay with my brothers. I want to have a family with a mum and a dad and brothers and sisters and eat cornflakes for breakfast, the one with the chicken on the front. Mum is so angry at me, I don't want to go home.'

'Your mum is not angry at you, Hope. She just doesn't understand.'

My head hurts. I can't deal with these questions any more.

'She is, she is, she hates me.'

I run from the room. Upstairs to my bed. I know the girls I share with are out for the day. They went out and I had to stay home because I had to have this meeting with the social worker. I slam the door and throw myself face down on the bed.

I don't want a bunch of people in a room talking about me when I'm not there. I want to be there. How do I know what they will say about me is true. Adults lie. Adults let you down. Adults never do what they say. Adults say things they don't mean. Oh please, I don't want to go home.

12

WARD OF COURT

News, 1983

The social worker is back. I see her car in the drive. The last time she was here, she left when I ran upstairs. They left me on my own for a bit, then Janet came up to get me. That was two sleeps ago. She spoke with me on her own, and gently asked me what I wanted.

'To go to the case conference.'

She explained that was not going to happen, but she was going on the 16th of December to see the judge, and she promised she would speak for me. She said, 'Your mum and dad will be there too.' That did it: I told her it was fine for her to go, and she had to tell the judge that I want to stay living here for now, and that I want to be fostered, with my brothers.

This morning, Craig and Janet were collected by the social worker. They were all wearing posh clothes. So even if Janet hadn't told me, I knew they were seeing the judge today. Everyone wears something nice to see a judge. I imagine my dad will wear his suit. Mum will wear her red blouse and leather skirt.

Since this morning I've had ants in my pants. Now they are back, I cannot bring myself to go downstairs and hear the news. Craig has called up the big staircase already:

'Hope, can you come downstairs, please?'

Maybe I can pretend I didn't hear. I just want to sit on my bed, chewing my lip.

There is a gentle knock on my bedroom door.

'Hope, it's OK. You and the boys, you are staying here.'

The relief floods from my body in the form of tears. By the time I've finished, I need a new pillow and a new pillowcase, as this one is soaked through. Craig calls them happy tears. These are the first happy tears I have ever cried.

Christmas Day, 1983

Even though we are Wards of Court, we are off home for Christmas. I don't understand.

I like Christmas, 'cos I know my dad saves all year with the off-licence for drink and crisps and nibbles and tiny pickled onions. There is always a Christmas table heaving with nuts, satsumas, chocolates, biscuits and lots of alcohol.

I am actually looking forward to seeing Mum and Dad. Harold and Jack are really excited about all the goodies Dad has promised us.

We are dressed in our new best clothes from Chesterfields. Even Mum notices when we get there. She is angry, I can tell by the tone of her voice.

'That's some nice clothes there you got. What ya

wearing 'em for, right up their arse, int ya? Hope, get the fucking things off.'

I walk off and leave her. She ain't upsetting me today.

There's a big plastic bag for each of us. Dad has drawn Santas on an old newspaper and placed one on each bag.

'That's your one, Hope. Jack that's yours and Harold's.'

None of the presents is wrapped, not like at Chesterfields, where there are lots of presents under the tree waiting for us when we get back. There's a big turkey too: Craig is saving some for us so I don't mind that Mum and Dad don't have a Christmas dinner for us. They never do.

The usual routine starts after the bags of presents are opened. Before we have a chance to say thanks, Elvis is being played on the record player and some dreary lovey-dovey songs are filling the room. My presents are all sweets this year. I eat as many as I can but keep some back to share with the other kids at Chesterfields who are not going home today.

'I knew that would happen.' Harold has crossed his arms and is really grumpy. We're on our way home, on Boxing Day.

'What?' I ask, although I know.

'Mum and Dad getting drunk, having a fight and spoiling our Christmas. Why do you have to pour them so many drinks, Hope? Going around lah de dah like a barmaid?'

'Dad likes me doing that, it makes him and Mum happy.'

'No it doesn't. They just get sick, cry to the music then puke everywhere. Then we have to clean it up,' says Jack.

Harold nods his agreement. 'It's not fair, I don't see why we have to go home for Christmas. It's rubbish. Mum and Dad are rubbish. Stupid music. Stupid drinking, stupid.'

School bus, 1984

We are still going to my old school. It's the first day back after Christmas. This morning was fun, getting on our very own big minibus early in the morning. Craig was driving us there, and we played games on the way. We three go to school the farthest away from Chesterfields – all the other children go nearby – so that means we get dropped off last and collected first.

I love school. I've almost caught up with everything I missed when we were living in the B&Bs. My teachers say I am bright and bubbly. Miss Watson was a bit confused when I asked her, all excited like, about the meaning of me being anxious. If I had known the meaning, I would have asked her in a different way, but then if I'd known the meaning, I wouldn't have needed to ask at all. Anxious is not a good thing to be, but according to the staff at Chesterfields Children's Home, it's what I am.

I hear Mum before I see her. It's home time and I'm about to get on the bus. She has turned up at school like this before. But now she is really pissed off 'cos we didn't go home for all of Christmas and we are now Wards of Court. Which means she doesn't look after us any more.

Not that she ever did.

'Please, Mum, please go away.'

'Aw fuckin' 'ell, 'ope. I just wanna see ya. They won't let me see ya.'

I jump past her onto the bus.

Where are the boys? Come on, boys, come on, let's go. I can't see them. Where are they? Mum, no, Mum.

'Mum, get off the bus, Mum, you ain't allowed, Mum. We can see ya on Sunday, right, Mum. Mum, get off the bus. Please, Mum.'

A wail of sirens announces the arrival of the coppers, which makes her even more determined to get on the bus. I can smell the whisky and fags on her.

No Mum, no.

There is a policeman at her back. Pulling her off the bus. I feel so sad that my heart is hurting. She loses a stiletto shoe, her hands are grabbing at the bus seats, at me.

'I just want to see my children. Please let me see ma kids. Please, please.'

The policeman hauls her out with one hand. Gets her shoe with the other. He hands it back to her, which seems to stop her fighting, or she is just resigned to fate.

My brothers are hiding in the door of the school. A teacher's protective frame in front of them, not letting them out, even if they wanted to run to Mummy.

I wish I was over there with the boys.

The copper speaks to her, gently now.

'There are designated times, Mrs Daniels, you know that. You can't just turn up here. Not at school. If you don't behave, they will stop you seeing them altogether.'

That gets her.

Alcohol takes over. She turns into a spitting cobra.

'No one can fuckin' tell me when I can and can't see me kids. They are mine. Mine. We ain't done fuck all wrong. Mine, I tell ya. Mine.'

'Mrs Daniels, please, we don't want you getting into any

more trouble, do we? If you go now and promise not to come back to the school, we can let the children go home and forget all about this breach of the peace.'

'Their home is over there, I tell ya. At the bottom of this street, not in poxy, fuckin' Highgate. Here. With me, with their dad. We know what's best. What the fuck are you all fuckin' lookin' at?'

A crowd of mothers collecting their children has gathered at the school gate. Only they can't collect them, as the teachers are keeping everyone inside until my mum fucks off.

The policeman is talking to her, moving her away. She is walking up the street. We wait to see if order can be restored. I watch her, one shoe on, one shoe off, hobbling down the middle of the road, swearing at the cars that almost hit her. Guilt wells in my tummy. She turns. Waves her shoe in the air. I wave back through the open door of the bus.

'It's all yer fuckin' fault this is, Hope, all yer doin'. I will never forgive ya, never.'

I stare after her.

I hate you, I hate you, I hate you. I wish you were dead. Everyone would feel sorry for me, but really I'd be glad. Glad that you can't do this to me no more.

My teacher's leaving, 1984

My teacher is off to a common. I am gutted. I've cried for days. I don't understand why she is leaving me. People always leave me.

What's at fuckin' Greenham Common that's so fuckin' important anyway? She's leaving because of me, I know she is. The trouble I brought to the class with Mum and Dad. Why is she leaving? She must have had enough of me. I am not going to get close to anyone ever again. They all just leave, so what's the point? I'm a horrid person that no one likes.

The TV repair man, 1984

We are home for a visit. My social worker tells me I have to come home, even if I don't want to. The doorbell rings. It's the Radio Rentals man here again. When I answer the door, he says he is here to fix the telly. I give him my best cold stare. I block the door.

'There is nothing wrong with the telly. Where you from? You've been 'ere before, why's the telly always broken? If it's that bad, why don't you give us a new one. The telly's crap, we need a new one, not for you to fix it. Fuck off.'

My dad is behind me, moving me away from the door. 'Now, now, Hope, let the nice man in. Upstairs, mate, you know where the telly is. The little woman's upstairs, she will show you where the TV is.' He winks.

Dad pushes us all into the living room and turns the telly on there.

He goes to the kitchen and gets some Cokes, a special treat. One for each of us.

'Shhh, Hope, don't tell yer brothers. There's somethin' special in it for ya.'

Another wink.

The taste is of coconut and Coke. It's so sweet, I love it.

'What is it, Dad?'

'Malibu, the Taste of Paradise. You finished that quick. Want some more?'

By the time my mum follows the TV man downstairs, stuffing notes in her bra, I am drunk, but I still know.

Dirty old fucker, dirty, dirty.

Notes, taken by Hope, in 1993, from social services files:
Nov 1984 – Letter from key worker at Chesterfields to my school in Hackney, asking do they think I should change school and go to a school near Chesterfields instead?

— Reply from school, Nov 1984, basically 'yes' but also:

— As wards of court – London Borough of Hackney is responsible for me and my brothers.

— Parents – way of life: bad. Unable and unwilling to take proper care of us. Inability and unwillingness of parents to change that mode of life.

Unwilling??? Nah, I don't believe it. They just didn't know how …

— No likelihood of us kids returning home to live with parents. V. good reasons for staying at Chesterfields and not foster homes 'cos – 1. Kids must stay together. 2. Parents and Phillip visit. 3. Strong bond between parents and children. 4. No foster parent could cope with the parents' behaviour.

— Hope likely to be living at Chesterfields until she is 18. Seems to have coped with everything very well – needs to be centred at Chesterfields, including schooling/out of school activities.

— Before Chesterfields – appallingly deprived and disturbed life. Important – the chance to grow up in as secure and supportive surroundings as possible.

Christmas Eve, 1984

I can't sleep . . . I am just too excited. I wonder if I will get the Duran Duran record I asked for – it is Christmas . . . Santa is coming. I know he's not real but the little kids here don't know that, so we still have to pretend. None of us really had Christmas before here, but if it's like last year, then it really happens.

I hope they don't let us down. I really really want 'The Wild Boys', it is just my favourite.

There are presents for me under the tree, but we aren't allowed to touch them until tomorrow. It's enough that I know they are there. My toes are flapping back and forth under the covers, not to warm them like I used to do at home, but just because my feet won't keep still and want to go and check which of the presents are for me.

Maybe I could sneak down and have a peek. No one will know.

The girls in my room are asleep, and the quiet of a big house full of people is comforting. The Christmas tree is at the bottom of the stairs, covered in lights and tinsel, and it is the biggest tree ever. There are a lot of 'biggests' this Christmas – the biggest turkey I've ever seen, crackers and party hats. There's the biggest pile of sprouts and carrots in the kitchen, minus one, which we have left out for Rudolf the red-nosed reindeer. I've never had sprouts. Maggie says they are 'yucky' but I will give them a go. They are green and I like green. We are also having croquette and roast potatoes. The last time we had croquettes, I had stolen them from the freezer in the corner shop. I didn't know what to do with them so we ate them frozen like ice lollies. Phillip got home just as we were halfway though, and went mad at us for eating frozen food. They tasted OK though.

Maggie wakes at a sound from downstairs. Sleepily, she announces: 'Santa's arrived.'

I hear her breathing go back to that of a person who is asleep.

It's not him. There are voices. A man and a woman. She's pissed off. I hope it is not my mother.

I sit up, tilt my head sideways to hear better, but I can't. I venture over to the bedroom door and open it a bit. The voices are definitely angry, and it is definitely not my mother.

Whew. Oooh who is it then?

The light from the hall makes Maggie turn, grumbling a little in her sleep, so I step outside.

Don't want to wake her up. I will get into trouble.

I am desperate to know who it is. Low but angry voices; another voice, which says, 'Calm down!' I sneak a look from the top of the stairs. The top of the Christmas tree provides me with a bit of cover. At the bottom of the stairs, there is Craig and his ex-wife – and they are arguing. There are a couple of coppers there too. The cops! They are all speaking in low voices, as if they are trying not to disturb us, but Craig looks really angry, and his ex-wife is accusing him of all sorts. She seems drunk. The coppers are telling her to calm down.

Oh no, oh no! I thought Craig was a nice man, she can't mean that about Craig. He can't have hit her. Oh no, oh no.

The Duran Duran record is forgotten. I am seriously worried Craig is not who he says he is.

Can I trust him now? No one else has said bad stuff about him, just this woman, and my mum. Has my mum caused this trouble with the wife? Oh no, oh no. Maybe he will take my presents away from me, 'cos my mum has caused this trouble.

I can't stand it any more. Will the coppers sort it? I know that copper: he always manages to calm my mum down, just before he puts her in the car and takes her away. Will they do the same to Craig? Will they be able to sort this out? If they catch me watching, I will be for it, and all my presents will be confiscated, Christmas or not.

I walk, backwards, to my room, not taking my eyes off the scene but knowing I shouldn't be there. I am scared that turning will mean I miss something or that a floorboard will creak. I lie awake for hours, thinking about Craig and his ex-wife. The trust I had in him has vanished.

Christmas morning dawns with the excitement of twenty children, few of whom knew about a proper Christmas until they started staying at Chesterfields. The volume of children's voices seems to be twice as high as on a normal morning, which is usually greeted with sleepy heads and grumbles about having to go to school.

Not today. Today there is chaos, kids running in and out of everyone's rooms. In the night, each of us has received a big sock filled with a tangerine, an apple, a chocolate bar and a 10p piece. We all know there are presents under the tree for us, and twenty children have never been so keen to eat their cornflakes.

There are happy squabbles: 'No, that's my bowl', 'That's my plate', 'Everyone eat quick, so we can get to our presents'.

'Slow down, kids, calm, calm. Walk, Maggie, don't run!'

I look up. I am relieved that Craig is still here, though a new feeling about him has appeared in the night. I am suspicious of him. He looks like nothing happened in the night. He looks like Craig always does. But I know he is pretending.

Duran Duran's 'The Wild Boys' is playing. Harold, Jack and I are jumping on my bed, dancing kind of in time to Simon Le Bon. My head is going from side to side and we are all pretending to play guitars and be the stars in the video.

Today I've discovered that I don't like sprouts, but I've seen Jack and Harold smile all day because this party doesn't mean booze or men coming round to the house to disappear with my mum.

Whatever I saw last night is far from my mind. Today was a good day, and for the first time in a long time, there is a new feeling – I don't know what it is, but I do know that today, for the first time in forever, I'm not anxious.

Chesterfields, Sunday 3 February 1985

I'm standing at the window upstairs waiting for Mum and Dad to visit. For once they are on time. I watch as Dad walks up to the gate of Chesterfields a few steps in front of Mum, and I can see she is bending his ear. His smile tells me that he ain't listening and this is going to be a nice day. As they walk through the gates they pass Julie and Craig, who are cleaning the minibus.

I hear Julie say, 'Good afternoon, Mr Daniels.' And Dad replies, 'Good Afternoon.'

Mum isn't so nice. She replies, 'Bloody awful afternoon.'

Mum barges through the door underneath the window I'm looking out of, so I run down the stairs to meet them, but it's too late. Mum and Dad are ignoring everyone else;

they are standing at the bottom of the stairs swearing at each other. I turn and stomp back up the stairs to my room.

Oh, for fuck's sake. What's the fuckin' point.

Notes, taken by Hope, in 1993, from social services files:
Report, Chesterfields, Sunday 3 February 1985

Hope – very upset. Ran upstairs crying as parents arrive and argue. Julie comforts her. Both come back downstairs to see parents.

Mum and Dad still arguing. Hope runs upstairs, crying again – still very upset.

Craig asks M&D – what's the problem? Mrs D immediately starts on him. Accuses Craig of all sorts i.e. 'You and your 16-year-old tart – that girl who's always up your bum.'

Craig reminds Mum of visiting arrangement – tells her she should behave. Dad, very embarrassed, takes Craig's side. Dad leaves.

Craig asks Mum to leave – she refuses, saying, 'Go on, get me nicked, then.'

Craig calls the coppers. I go back downstairs – see police escort. Mum taken away – she doesn't cause too much trouble with the police, but does carry on making allegations against Craig.

Julie takes me upstairs. I am still very upset. Julie is kind and comforting. I tell her Mum is having a go at Craig and Chesterfields, complaining all the time about my new bedroom.

This is the worst incident so far. Upset before though. Said I don't want to see M&D anymore or have them visit again. Told Julie that M&D often drunk when they turn up at school in the mornings/lunchtime.

Further chat – tell Julie that my parents are getting worse. Go for a walk on the heath – me & Julie. Also tell her Mum came to school drunk the Monday before and Jack hid inside, worried in case the headmistress came and saw parents drunk. Julie reassured me: Jack and Harold and me now safe. I said, 'But Mum and Dad aren't safe.' Report says I said this several times.

I share details of the many fights, rows, at home before we came into care – frightened they will have another row here.

Jack and Harold tell staff they haven't seen me cry so much over my parents for a long time. Staff got me to think of some positive things before going to bed. Me and the boys got hot chocolate. Said I was okay, just wanted a cuddle.

I remember that day. Well, I remember Mum and Dad arriving, the fight, running upstairs, the police, talking to the staff. Mum! All those things you said!

13

FAVOURITES

Betty's house, 1985

The younger kids are in and out of the flat on the first floor like yo-yos. It's Betty's flat. Along with Craig she is one of the other residential social workers that looks after us kids. Everyone has been very nice to the boys and me since Mum kicked off – except Betty. Betty was never nice to me, since the day I met her. The other girls say she likes the little kids more than the older ones anyway. I'm only ten, which is not very big, yet she still doesn't like me. It's not fair.

I'm sitting outside the living-room, as I sometimes do, just like I used to sit outside the kitchen at home. Betty and Cathy are in there with some adults. Two of them, a man and a woman. They look nice. Their clothes are ironed and clean. The women's hair is perfect. They look a bit nervous though. Cathy and I share a room, but I want to be fostered more than her. After lights out we sometimes list all the reasons we want to be fostered first. I always win by a mile. So I don't understand why Betty and Cathy are in the room and I'm not. I heard Betty introduce Cathy to the adults:

'Cathy, these are your new foster parents.'

I imagine she said, 'Hope, these are your new foster parents.' But she didn't, because I know Betty doesn't like me and doesn't want me to get what I want. That makes me feel all funny inside.

I'm not allowed into Betty's flat, but the little kids are. I watch the little kids disappear through the big yellow fire door and past her welcoming smile. She has made cakes in there, I know she has. The little ones go in and play. But I'm excited, as she has invited us all to her house in Barnet at the weekend.

The bus jerks forward out of the gates of Chesterfields. I stare at the new buds on the trees.

How clever the trees are: they change colour, drop their leaves and then start to grow again. Conkers soon! I wish I could get Mum to re-grow like that.

As we drive closer to Barnet, I notice that some of the shops on either side of the street are boarded up. The *Evening Standard* says, 'Mandela Rejects Offer of Freedom'.

I must remember to ask Julie: 'Who's Mandela? Why would anyone reject freedom?' Better not ask Betty now, as I am only on this bus 'cos I've been on me best behaviour.

The house is mid-terrace, a bit like in *Coronation Street*, but more London. There are two floors and inside it is super clean. It smells nicer than a beef pie. It's the first time I have been here, but the littler ones have obviously been here before, because they head straight for the juice in the kitchen. I stay in the room with the sofa. It's very flowery. All the walls and the chairs have flowers on them. There are lots of pictures of old people, none of friends, or people Betty's age, no children or a husband. Some of the women in the photos look like Betty, but with wrinkles.

I can see everyone in the garden, wrapped up warm, and the kids screaming with delight at the idea of petting the neighbour's rabbit.

'You're to be careful, kids, don't hurt him. He needs quiet.'

They all troop through the gate in the low fence to next door. I decide to follow, but Betty is standing in the door-way, stopping me from joining the others.

'Hope, what are you doing in here?'

'Nothing, Betty. Excuse me, I am just going to join the others.'

'I don't think so, Hope. As you like it so much in here to be snooping around, you can sit there on the sofa and not move. Now, Hope.'

That was a tone of voice that I know is not to be messed with. The kind of voice that says, I'm the adult and there will be trouble if you don't learn the rules and do as you are told. The kind of voice that scares you, a voice that you know is strong enough to hate you.

I sit on the sofa.

'Right, stay there until we are ready to go home.'

I don't protest. I just sit.

She has told the others how horrid I am. She has told them she doesn't like me, so they aren't to play with me. They are all playing outside and Betty won't let me join in. It's not fair, it's not fair. I wish she would leave and disappear and never come back. Never.

Never. She is a cow for hating me. I want to be back at Chesterfields and not here, in this smelly house, on this stupid sofa, with her stupid photos of stupid old people while she is out there playing with everyone, telling them how horrid she thinks I am.

More and more as I grow, I have trouble getting what is inside of my head outside of my mouth. A thought gets in my head and there it sticks. When we get back to Chesterfields, still my head feels heavy, and thoughts of how much Betty hates me just won't go away. Stuck in my throat, pushing backwards up and into my head. I can't speak, so to try and stop the thoughts whirring round my head, sometimes I just stamp my feet and slam doors. It doesn't work, though. The thoughts are still there and they stay there until night-time, so I can't sleep sometimes, even when they give me hot chocolate and let me stay up until I feel a bit better. It feels like everyone hates me. Except Julie, my key worker. Julie says I must try to talk about stuff, not just 'go off on one'. But there is so much 'stuff' I am scared to talk about it.

What happens if I start talking and I can't stop? They will all hate me more, that's what'll happen – 'cos of what happened at home. I won't get fostered and they will make me leave here. Who wants a girl who's done all that stealing? What happens if I start speaking and it all comes tumbling out, and they think I did a bad job with the boys? They will find out . . . they will find out all about lots of stuff . . . I just can't tell them, I just can't.

I lie down on my bed. A memory of a man and the cross of Jesus tries to come back to me. It feels as if it's happening again, now. He's there in front of me, with Mum, on the bed, and I know he's not, but it feels like it's real, I can really see him. Like I'm back there. Bounce, bounce,

bounce. I shake my head so the man doing dirty things with my mum isn't there any more. But he doesn't go, until he has finished. My head hurts. I stand up.

I want to be outside, not stuck in here. It will be better when we're fostered, then we'll be part of a real family and eat Kellogg's cornflakes for breakfast. No one has to know anything then.

I slam the bedroom door behind me and run downstairs into the garden. I sit on top of the climbing frame, letting the thoughts swirl in time to the wind. I imagine the wind going through my ears into my head and out the other side, taking the thoughts away. Out of the corner of my eye, I see the staff checking on me through the window. I won't look, I won't look, I won't look. I sit on the top of the frame, waiting for new leaves on the trees to appear. I wait for the wind to clear the inside of my head. I am waiting for spring.

Floating, 1985

Oh, this is nice. Troubles are floating away. All them thoughts about hating school. All them kids who do nothing but talk about their holidays and mums and dads, after school clubs, are all way below me and I am floating.

It's good this stuff. Sniff the lid of the aerosol can and no one knows any more that my mum is a prossie, and even if they do I don't give a flying fuck, 'cos I am flying. I must get more of this stuff. The whole world of worries floats away on an aerosol can. It sprays into the lid and all the crap drifts away.

Bedroom, 1985

My bedroom is pink. I still cannot believe how nice it is. I do my bit by trying to keep it tidy. I make my bed every day, and even though some days I just want to go to bed really early and not get up, I have to. Mum and Dad still turn up at school drunk: Dad tries to tell everyone in the playground jokes, which everyone finds funny except me and the teachers.

I now share my bedroom with Megan and Maggie. They are both two years younger than me, so it's like I am the mum of the room. I spend hours in there, playing and plaiting their hair. I cornrow their hair, like the black girls in Hackney do. It looks good once it's done but I have to concentrate on all the steps that my school friend showed me to make sure I do it properly.

We all sit on Maggie's bed. We don't sit on my bed as it's well made and it's mine. First, I am careful to comb their hair through, getting rid of all the tangles. It's better if the hair is a little wet, and then I put it into bunches. I pull out a little bit of a bunch and divide it again into three, plaiting the strands over each other. I keep on plaiting in little new strands of hair all the way down the row, making a neat, tight braid. At the end, we snap the bead in, or sometimes a hairclip. Rubber bands aren't any good: I used them once and Maggie's hair seemed to get caught up in it and snap.

We spend hours in our room, after school and at weekends, doing stuff. We play until we are called for our dinner. It feels like I have sisters. It feels like heaven.

Potential, 1985
We are moving schools. Mum and Dad won't turn up any more and make me want to hide my head under the desk.

I got my Easter report card from school and it says I am catching up. I am also very bright but get too easily distracted. No shit! I have to learn not to talk in class when the teacher is talking. The card says I have potential. I had to look that up in the dictionary. Julie and Craig actually read the report. They didn't chuck it straight in the bin like Mum did when we lived at home.

Last night it was a whole month since I stopped wetting the bed in my sleep. Julie and Craig are very proud of me. They both smiled and Craig put his hand on top of my head and messed up my hair until I laughed out loud.

The even better news today is that the witch Betty is leaving. I am so happy when I hear this from Craig that I dance around the garden; I dance and dance until Craig sticks his head out the back door and tells me to come inside because it is 'unladylike for me to be screaming at the top of my voice!'

'Hurrah, hurrah, the witch is leaving!'

But I know from the way he told me that he is also happy the witch is leaving.

Summer holiday, July 1985

Live Aid is on the telly, and we're waiting for Duran Duran. I'm so excited I'm scared I'm going to pee my pants. I'm going to marry Roger Taylor. I was going to marry Simon Le Bon, but he got married.

Earlier this month we went on holiday, on a plane! It was great fun and I didn't have to talk to adults about what was going on in my head for two whole weeks. They were still really nice to us, all the staff. Kind and caring, never shouting. But for two whole weeks no one asked me if I was OK in that way they do when they put their head to one side, change their voice and say, 'Are you OK, Hope, are you getting the right support?' Like I'm meant to be telling them some deep dark secret. Us kids, we mimic this saying more than anything else. But on holiday we didn't have to, because it was the question that was never asked. For two whole weeks they never asked me in that soft voice, and if they had, I could've answered that I felt OK and I had no need for the aerosol.

There were fewer rules while we were away, and while I liked cleaning my shoes on a Sunday, and leaving them to dry by the radiator, it was fun not having a set bedtime for a bit, and spending all the pocket money we'd saved for going away.

Even though we got a lecture because 'You all pushed the boundaries' by going to the disco until after midnight, the staff on holiday with us were just cool. They sat down with us and laughed with us, before they firmly explained how it was important to them that they could trust us and that we didn't let them down.

They asked if they had ever broken their promises to us. None of us could think of a single time. So at the meeting, they said that all they were asking was the same of us. I liked that.

New school, 1985

My new school is shit. The teachers are shit, and the other kids are shit. They are all posh and talk about stuff I don't know about, like holidays with their families, new bikes and clubs they go to, piano lessons and stupid stuff like that.

The only good thing about it is my friend, Erica. She has a great mum, called Alice. Alice listens to me and lets me come round their house.

Erica and I met 'cos we were sitting next to each other in our class. She was the first person to ask me why I take a can of deodorant into school and hide it up my sleeve.

I just told her, 'I have it 'cos I sniff it in maths to shut my head up. Why, what do you do to sort ya head out?'

'Listen to Duran Duran and Culture Club.'

'Oh.'

'Wanna come over to meet my mum and listen to records sometime?'

'OK. Can I bring my "Wild Boys" record?'

'Sure.'

I look down and laugh at the aerosol can. We both laugh. 'Sure' is the brand of deodorant I am holding.

I head home smiling. I haven't had a sniff all day.

14

A MOTHER'S INFLUENCE

Helping Mum, 1986

'Hope, Hope, come here, Hope.'

I move towards my mother. The last couple of times, she has been OK on visits. Not as quiet as the other parents, but OK. I automatically smell her to see if she has been drinking. She has.

'Hope, Hope. We was finkin', ya dad and me, that how you're getting so fat, and the boys tell us that there's more food here than in the supermarket . . . Well, Hope, Hope . . . We was finkin' that, you know, you could help us out like. It's tough at home, you know. A few bits and bobs like, you can get it like from the cupboard. No one will notice. It's OK, Hope. No one will care. There is so much here.'

She looks at me, eyes wide, hopeful. I look down.

I don't want to do this. They are nice to me here, I don't want to be thrown out, but I want to make her happy. Maybe she will love me again if I do it.

I look up. In the silence, her tone of voice hardens slightly, but she is still smiling:

'Come on, Hope . . . Love, it is you who got us into this mess. The least you can do is help ya mum and dad out with a bit o' food? Eh?'

'OK, Mum, OK. I'll do it.'

'That a girl, I knew you wouldn't let yer ol' mum and dad down.'

I turn to go. Her voice changes from nectar to something else.

'Oh, and don't forget something for the cat.' She cackles. My heart goes from light to heavy in a second.

That bloody cat gets treated better than we ever did. Not fair, not fair.

A can of Coke, 1986

I'm looking forward to seeing my social worker. She's coming over tomorrow after school. I've been feeling a bit odd lately and I want to speak to her about it. I feel like Mum and Dad are getting worse and something's going to happen.

She is taking me out for tea. She doesn't come to visit anyone else, just me. It's really nice. I don't have to share her with anyone. She just comes to see me, and just takes me out to tea. She leaves everyone else at home and takes me out.

There are big windows with a seat in them in the living room, and I'm sitting there looking out, when I see my mother. She staggers up holding the can of Coke that seems attached to her arm and I know is full of whisky and not much Coke.

Shit, I can't believe it, what's she doin' 'ere? She looks angry and that means trouble.

'Craig, Craig, help quick, me mum is here and she looks mad. Don't let the other kids see her, she will scare them, Craig, I don't want her to scare them again. Stop her, Craig. Quick! Quick!'

We run out to the front path from the side door. Too late. My mum is almost at the front door. I hide behind Craig, hoping she'll disappear, fall down dead. Make life easier.

'Mrs Daniels?' Craig calls to her. She reacts like he is a red rag to a bull. Spinning on her heels, she charges towards him, kicking, screaming at him:

'You bastard, you bastard! You are a nonce, you know that, a fuckin' nonce!'

I don't know what she means, but as Craig is repeatedly calling for someone to ring the police, I can guess that calling him a nonce – even though it's her favourite word for him – isn't the best thing she could do.

Oh shit! Oh Shit! Oh shit!

'Come on, Hope. Come on, kids, come on. Upstairs, all of you. Quick, all of you. Hope, come on. Now!' calls Julie from the hallway.

'Julie, what's going on?'

'Don't worry, Hope, come on. Come on, all of you, in here.'

We are ushered like chicks by a hen into the private flat on the first floor. The door closes behind us, but I cannot sit still.

'Shit, shit, shit. What is she doing?'

I rush to the window and open it. Outside, Mum is almost

bent double, staggering a bit, the Coke can still in her hand. She is waving it about, between herself and Craig.

'I know what you do with the girls, you dirty fucker.'

She spits as she speaks; she sways, backwards and forwards. Her feet totter, as if she's trying to dance in time with music that's not playing. The only sounds are my mother making all sorts of accusations against Craig and Craig trying to pacify her. I am fixated on her feet. Left foot forward, then both feet stumble backwards. Somehow she is keeping her balance, the Coke can stretched out in front providing a counterweight to the unbalancing pull of whisky.

Not again, Mum, not again. Go away, go away, go away.

I've heard her accuse Craig before, but this time she seems more vicious than ever, releasing her venom, building suspicion around a man who has shown me nothing but kindness and support.

I watch as she carries on kicking him, screaming, calling him the same names, over and over. The other kids are watching her too.

One of her high-heeled shoes is off and I watch as she whacks him with it. His arm is up, covering his face. She scratches and spits at him.

I want to die. I hate her so much. Why is she coming into this home and bringing evil to it?

Police sirens cut a swathe through the streets. As the coppers get out of the car, she lunges once again towards Craig. Her nails connect with his face as she takes hold of his hair, scratches and kicks him. As the coppers pull her away, she is still kicking, her arms flying around, but the coppers know what they are doing and, as she is bundled into their car, all she connects with is thin air.

I stare down at the car as it does a three-point turn before leaving. Voices behind me must have forgotten who she is, or that I am there:

'That'll be the last straw, she'll be banned now.'

'Yep.'

I run to my room. Sobbing and crying. The pain hurts so much.

I hate her. I hate her. I want the pain to stop. I want my mother to die, and then I can be happy.

Bingo, 1986

Mum seems to have accepted that we are staying in care. She has shut up about it being my fault, and ever since she got banned from visiting Chesterfields, she seems a bit better, calmer. We are still allowed to visit them at home. She is still drinking, but the men aren't there when we visit and she doesn't do my head in as much.

She's upstairs with the boys, in her room, watching telly. I like this 'cos it leaves me and Dad alone, to do our thing. He has saved the bingo numbers for me from the *Sun*, and we are playing now. I call the numbers and he is marking them off on his card, a running commentary of how he is getting on:

'Two fat ladies, 88.'

'No.'

'Rise and shine, 29.'

'Yes!'

'Young and keen, 15.'

'Yes!'

'That's all the numbers, Dad, have we won?'

'No.'

It's the same every week, just different numbers. The excitement, the build-up, then the realization that actually no, we haven't won anything. I look at my dad, and welcome the routine we never had when we lived here.

First, we check the *Hackney Gazette*, for the local jumble sales.

'This one, Hope.'

'No this one, Dad.'

'This is the best one, Hope, I think we should go there. Last week that one was shite.'

'OK, Dad, let's go to this one.'

'OK, but first . . . What do you think I have for you this week?'

He disappears into the kitchen and I follow. I like the way the sun always manages to brighten this room up, so even though the paint on the walls, the cupboards and the ceiling still need fixing after the fire that swept through the house before the council moved us in, it's an OK room.

On a plate on the table, under a cloth, there is a pile of something.

'What is it, Dad? What have you got us?'

'Oh something sweet like you, Hope.'

'Oh, Daddy, what is it?'

I reach out to pull the cloth, but my hand is tapped away. Dad reaches to lift the cover himself, a magician. He does the actions, says the magic word.

'Abracadabra.'

'Doughnuts! With sugar! Oh thanks, Dad!'

How good is this!

My share is gone before the boys can be called from upstairs for this treat. My mouth covered with sugar and jam. I go to the mirror and lick it all off, making sure nothing is left, a bit sorry that I ate mine so quickly and I've none left. I can't have another one, even though I want one. The boys run in, eyes wide, and without saying a word eat theirs just as quickly, in case they disappear or, if they leave them long enough, they will find out the sugary jam doughnuts aren't real.

We are satisfied, but Dad has not finished. On each chair there is a carrier bag for each of us, full of stuff he has nicked. I pick up my bag and take it into the living room to pour the contents on the floor. It's all there . . . every *Hackney Gazette* saved since our last visit – which, by the date on the oldest one, was three months ago. I love the *Hackney Gazette*. 'The Hackney' is its nickname, which always reminds me of home, of it being ripped up into squares for toilet paper, and trying to piece the squares together to read them. There are also magazines: this time he has got me *Jackie*! There is Impulse deodorant and a bottle of shampoo and there are loads of sweets – Refreshers, sugar necklaces, gum – anything that can fit in a hand and then be slipped into a pocket without anyone seeing.

I wish I could steal like my dad.

Once the bags are done, Mum and the boys once again disappear upstairs to watch the telly, leaving Dad and me in bliss to play bingo, which we never win, and plan the afternoon's telly – today, as usual, we choose wrestling and *The A-Team*.

Days such as these were few and far between, but that doesn't make them any less special. I am grateful for these warm memories of such times with my dad. The only problem with these nice memories is that bad memories follow to shatter the good thoughts. Always, at the end of these nice days, I remember the knock on the door, which brought the boys down, and the man from 'Radio Rentals' climbing upstairs to fix the telly in my mum's room, with Dad saying, 'Yer mum's supervising his work.' He came even though the telly had been working properly all day. I knew he wasn't from Radio Rentals: it was the regular, Gary, who Mum and Dad pretended was a normal friend. I don't know why they pretended. The court had told them that we knew that the men came to the house to do dirty things to my mum. They each arrived with a bottle of whisky and a smelly smile that tarnished my day.

Julie's leaving, 1987

I am sitting outside the kitchen door, unable to kick the habit of listening in to other people's conversations.

Well, how else are you meant to know what goes on here. No one tells no one nothing.

'So what about Julie leaving, then? Such a shame she is so ill like that.'

What! No. No. No. She's mine. My care worker, she can't leave. She's the one I trust. She can't be ill. She is the only one who fights for me when I've been bad, and gives me hugs when I am sad. Julie! She can't leave, she can't.

This time they are going to have to tell me what is going on. I slam into the kitchen, the door swinging on its hinges, demanding:

'Why is Julie leaving?'

'Hope, what did you hear?' It's Craig.

'You said she was leaving. She can't leave.'

Craig smiles. 'On holiday, Hope, she is going on holiday.'

My eyes burn through him. I know he's lying. I'm stunned.

I don't know it yet, but soon Julie will leave and I will never see her again. I've never known why. Whatever did happen to her, Craig definitely lied, or else it was a very long holiday. Not knowing why people leave you is harsh and it stays with you your whole life.

An outing, 1987

We're off to the cinema and then to McDonald's with Mum and Dad. Although we know we aren't really. Mum and Dad are given the money to take us, but when we get back we shall have to lie to Craig about where we've been and what we've seen.

A taxi picks us up and takes us to the big cinema on Holloway Road to avoid Mum having a fight with the staff at the care home. We stand there until they arrive. Steered away from the cinema, we get the McDonald's but Mum and Dad don't eat. They collude with us, joke and threaten us into a big fat lie.

'Right,' says Dad, 'pretend I'm Craig and I ask you, "What did you see at the cinema?"'

'Nothing, Dad. We didn't go, Dad.'

'Nooo. You have to say you went and saw *Grease*.'

'But we saw *Grease* before, Dad.'

'Well tell the fucker you've seen it again.'

Harold moans.

'Start again. Right, I'm Craig. "What did you see at the cinema?"'

'*Grease*.'

'That's it, perfect, but don't look so damn guilty. You got

yer McDonald's, didn't yah? Better to be 'ere, chattin' with yer ol' mum and dad, rather than being in some poxy cinema watchin' a film you've already seen – right?'

'Right,' we reply in unison.

By the end of the McDonald's I don't think of it as a lie. It's just something we do, so Mum and Dad can take the cinema money and spend it on drink.

New staff, 1987

When I wake up this morning, the sun is shining. I'm lying in bed eyes shut, feeling warm and safe.

How lucky am I? The staff here are really like big brothers and sisters to me and feeling not-anxious is really nice.

The sounds of summer call me from outside the window reminding me it is the start of the school summer holidays and my thirteenth birthday – plus Mum not being allowed to come to the home any more – everything has been super-OK for ages and ages. I no longer wet the bed, and haven't for a whole year. My report card from school is getting better and better each term. It says I'm doing well and the stability since I changed schools is obviously helping me, but I've to keep trying as I'm still not working to my full potential.

Craig had a chat with me about this last night. It's OK though, 'cos he explained that even though I want to make sure everyone likes me, and I'm very helpful around the home, everyone is very fond of me, and they are there to support me doing better. I have to be myself and not be worried about pleasing other people all the time. I thought a lot about that last night before I went to sleep. It is the first thing I think about when I wake up, that and the summer holidays!

Craig is right, I need to look after me first, then others. Focus on school when I go back, but right now it's the holidays! Right, time to get up.

I clatter down the stairs. There's a woman in the kitchen I don't recognise.

'Who are you? Where's Craig?'

'I'm Penny. Craig's not here anymore,' she says.

'What? How come?'

'Erm, you'll need to ask the new head of the home. She'll be here at 9 a.m. You will know her; she used to work here. She's called Betty.'

'Shit.'

'Excuse me, young lady, what is your name?'

'Hope.'

'Right, less of the swearing please. Now get your breakfast without another word.'

'But where's the rest of the staff?'

'Not another word. They have all gone. There will be agency staff until Betty gets her new team together.'

Betty, shit, the witch is back. Maybe it's not the same Betty. It has to be, there isn't another Betty that worked here. Oh fuck. What's going on? What's going on? Why won't they tell us? Where is Craig, where is Julie? Why did they leave without saying goodbye? They wouldn't do that. Why? Why? Why?

My fist thumps against the wall. All the faces of the adults are new: there isn't one adult here that I know, that I can trust. I've only just started trusting the others properly, and then they leave.

Oh what have I done? I know they will have left because of me.

It's my fault, it must be my fault. Everyone always leaves because of me.

There is a great pain in my chest. It feels tight. It's stabbing me. I feel so alone, so abandoned.

I don't like this change. I feel suffocated. I don't want to see the witch Betty. She hates me. She has her favourites. A feeling sweeps over and into me. I feel I have to leave, get out of here, before she comes. Where have they gone? Why have they left me here alone? Oh what am I going to do? Why won't anyone tell me?

To this day, neither I nor the other kids have ever found out why they left so suddenly.

I feel a bit funny. *I shouldn't have drunk so much.* I'm in a black cab from the West End of London. I'm on my way home to Chesterfields, to see if the witch, Betty, has arrived and pushed everyone out. I don't have any money to pay for the cab.

She can bloody well pay for it. She said I will turn into my mother. Well, I will show her, she can pay for the cab 'cos I've no money. It's her fault my lovely staff have left me alone. She will have driven them away so she can run the home for herself, give attention to all her favourites. I haven't told the driver I've no money. Ooops! I better not be sick. Oh, mind the corners, mister.

Even though I'm drunk and I have no more money to pay for the taxi, I figure it'll be OK and the home will pay.

15

THE PHOTOGRAPH

In the paper, 1987
'Look. Look, Hope.' My social worker hands me the newspaper. 'Do you want a cup of tea?'

I nod, unable to believe it, that there I am, in the paper.
Page 13, top right-hand corner.

Is that a good place to be?

It's me. I'm in the nationals. It's not like before, when
Mum was in the paper and Dad tried to hide it from us.

I read the words under my photograph: 'Will you foster
this child?' I'm staring out at myself.

They have given me a false name: Michelle. Michelle
is thirteen. Michelle is blonde. Michelle is looking for
the love of a good family. She needs support and a stable
environment. She is intelligent. She is looking back at
me, and she's looking at all the people that will foster
me. They are looking at her, too. I know they are. I move
the paper to an inch in front of my face so our eyes are
level. I'm staring at her closely, hoping I cannot see her

secrets. Has Michelle hidden them well? It's like looking in a mirror.

Butterflies raise excitement that tingles from the base of my tummy, up my middle and into my mouth. Forcing it open into a smile. My back straightens with pride as my grin pushes outwards to reach my ears. My teeth, which cannot be seen in the photograph, are revealing themselves to Michelle. Happiness helps me hold my chin high, and I feel the sparkle in my eyes. Bright with possibility, looking forward, imagining the family that will take me in, the pink bedroom with soft blankets, my own wardrobe, from where I can put down roots. A place where I don't have to pack everything into boxes every month or so. A place where things will not get lost. A place for Bros music and posters of Duran Duran. Laughter. Kindness. Nice dinners. Food that doesn't have to be shared. Someone to set rules for me. Buy me clothes and let me go out. A place I want to come home to.

A place where I no longer have to rebel by doing the very things that let me and everyone else down. Rebellion by living up to people's worst expectations. Doing the exact things people expect of the stereotypical definition of a person in care. Here, with this advert, I have a chance to change! To be someone. A chance to rewrite the stereotype, alter the low expectations other people have of me.

With foster care I can be something, someone. My new foster home will be somewhere I am no longer scared, no longer hurting. No longer wanting to cut. A place where I can release my feelings the way other people do – rather than in private, by cutting my own skin. No longer needing to go through the ritual. A knife placed along my thighs to release the tension that builds up with responsibility. A mechanism to cope with fear and the complex emotions that I don't know how to handle. Feelings that build like a boiling kettle but disappear into the atmosphere with my knife as it cuts into the surface of my skin. An inch, six inches. A place, perhaps, where I no longer feel compelled to do this, where I can cope with myself. A place where I can begin to like myself again. My head sinks. The smile has gone. The social worker is talking with someone outside the room. I am left alone with my dreams.

I spread the paper on the table. Not taking my eyes off Michelle for even a second, I search her face, tilt my head, and imagine the people who read *The Times*.

Do they sleep well at night?

I look at her and wonder how the paper with her picture will be waiting for them. It will lie in their hallway, at the bottom of the stairs. They are rich enough to have their newspaper delivered. Light is streaming through the window above their front door. White clean walls with black and white photos. Smiling happy people watch from the picture frames as she pads downstairs in warm slippers and a dressing gown to pick up the paper from the doormat. She is modern. She turns the paper over in her hands, looking at the headlines first and then the bottom of the front page. She does not look at the sports pages. She reads as she walks; reads about Julian Knight who is nineteen. How he goes on a shooting rampage in Melbourne, killing seven people and injuring nineteen before surrendering to police.

A nice Victorian hallway, with original cornicing, painted last year, down a couple of steps to the kitchen and breakfast room. She has a whole room just to eat breakfast in. The butter is in a dish and her husband follows her into the room, smiling at his wife. Hair sticking up. He makes breakfast as she reads the paper. He places tea, toast and orange juice on the table. Maybe fruit. I can almost smell the fresh coffee. They have time to sit and read the paper. She gives him the sports pages and the business pages and the front page. They share the paper. She gets to page 13 and there I am, as Michelle, staring out at her. Her life has suddenly changed and she knows it. For the rest of the day, week, they discuss fostering.

The person who sees me, who will take me in, who will be my foster parent, will want to foster because of my photograph. I can change their life. I imagine that, having seen me, they will be unable to sleep until they help me. The couple agree to start the process. Over the next few weeks, they – along with dozens of others – will write in because they want to help me. In the photograph, I am smiling, although I have a spot on the bottom of my chin. I look closely. I am now despondent.

Oh shit, I have a spot.

Ten minutes after the social worker leaves, I am pacing my room like a caged animal. The worry has borne down on me. No one will want me, because the spot will show them that I'm not worthy of their love or care. I pace, turn on my heels, hands pressed together. I am rubbing them distractedly, staring at nothing. I catch myself in the mirror and realise that no one will love me. No one has before. Why should they start now? I cannot cry. The pressure. The pressure. I feel myself heating up. I press my hands against my head.

Make it go away. Make it go away.

Images of that man on top of my mother. My mother screaming at me.

Bitch. Useless. Ugly. Waste of space. Fucking cunt.

If you hear something often enough, you believe it. I am sitting on my bed now. Rocking backwards and forwards. There are no tears. My hands are grabbing at my hair; I am rubbing my hands flat against my head, not caring that my hair is becoming a tangled mess. It's more important to me to try and pull these terrible memories out of my head.

The smell of my wet bed. The lice. My brother left us. My sisters left us. The attack on the house. No one loves me, because I did something bad. I don't know what, but my mother told me I don't deserve anything, am better off getting out of her way.

Get out of my fucking face, you little runt, if you know what is good for you.

Whisky. Cigarettes. Smoke. The strange brothers that became my mother's friends. One of them grabbing her breast. Dad watching, saying nothing. Not moving. Not protecting her. Letting them go upstairs. Dad staying downstairs. The floorboard creaks as she steps on it.

Hope, you will turn out just like your mother.

I want to cry, but I can't. I am heating up, and my head is filling up so the front of my face feels like it's being pounded from within. At the same time, the rest of my body feels numb with the pressure. It's like there are two of me. One is screaming, throwing all sorts of memories at me, reconfirming that I am worth nothing. I cannot even voice to myself what's hurting me because I've pushed all those feelings into a dark place, deep inside me. When I feel like this it's like those feelings push to escape, like they're wanting out from the place I've pushed them. Every time I'm hurt, I turn those feelings in on myself, like I've created a little person, and I push her and her feelings deeper into myself. Locking my hurt so far away I cannot, am unable, to speak about it any more.

On days like today, when she escapes and reminds me how rubbish I am, she runs round my insides screaming to get out. Pressure. Pressure builds. My head feels like it's going to explode. I need the release. However much I try to avoid it. The pressure, the pressure. I feel like I will black out if I can't get to my kit in time. I feel like I may harm myself by jumping off a bridge if I can't get these feelings out of me. I can't express them, but I can't cope with them either. I need them out, I want them out. It's the same every time.

I don't remember getting my kit out of the back of my underwear drawer. But it's there beside me. From some- where else, I let the person who normally hides deep inside me reach out. She opens the box – it's my hand, but it feels like someone else. My hand opens the box. Inside is my kit. Tissues, antiseptic wipes and a bandage. Underneath these is my knife. I pick it up, clean the knife with an antiseptic wipe. I lift my skirt. I press the knife to my thigh and push through the pain. I want, need the relief to overtake me. It's the only way I know how to cope. Releasing the pres- sure by the cut, I only feel the pain at first, before it's over- taken by relief, by euphoric feelings that wipe away the pain and self-loathing that I carry around with me and cannot talk about or let go. This is the only thing I have found that works; this cutting is the thing that helps me cope, keeps me alive.

The blood flows from my leg, taking with it the pressures, the fears, the unkind words and horror of my early childhood. I feel them flow out of me. I have created the cut that lets them go. It's a physical action that gives me mental relief. The more the blood pumps, the more I'm able to release myself from the demons that live in my head. The greater is my ability to cope with the rest of the day.

When the mental high I get from cutting subsides, I come back to myself. I put pressure on the wound. Clean myself up. Wipe everything down. No sign of my secret. I lie on my bed for a moment, looking at George Michael and Andrew Ridgeley, thinking how perfect their lives are. I'm not jealous because I am in love with them, especially George.

'Wham!' I shout out loud before standing up, slowly, to go back downstairs. Under their watchful eyes I place my box of tricks safely at the back of my drawer. I smile at them, knowing I'm once again strong enough to face the rest of my day.

Protesting, 1987

Apparently I've become what my social worker calls a 'chronic absconder'. They think I actually care. They cannot understand why I run away, but I can. I can't stand being at home with the witch. She hates me, but that's OK 'cos I hate her too.

All the lovely staff have gone and we've been told they're not coming back. We have not been told why. My world has been turned upside down and right now it's like a great big pile of messy clothes that need sorting. Betty tries to speak to me, but she only ends up telling me off and saying she doesn't understand me. She's worried about what I do when I run away. She knows I go to the West End 'cos I always get a black cab home, which she pays for – every time.

The West End of London is great. Sometimes I stay overnight, just walking; my head feels so full that sometimes it takes all night to clear. Other times I go back to the home.

I take the bus into town and my excitement builds with each stop. The lights of Piccadilly welcome me as I jump off at the Eros statue, always smiling at the god of love, waiting for him to find me. The walk through Leicester Square and by the cinema my mum and dad met at is done quickly. The regulars who look out for me let me pass today with a wave. Chinatown greets me with its red and gold gates and the smell of duck and spices that fills my nostrils.

It's just fab 'ere.

I'm keen to get to Trafalgar Square. This is the place I know, where I go every time I come to town. It's where I meet my friends on the Nelson Mandela picket line. They have been here every day and night since before I went into care. That is a long time. They let me help out, and I feel like I belong here. They're fighting for something they believe in, and that has to be good.

Today's a little bit different though. First of all, they are OK. The usual 'Hello, Hope, how you doin'?' or 'All right, Hope?'

Then something changes.

'What the fuck is that, Hope?'

He grabs my hand, tight, and lifts it up.

'Ow, you are hurting my arm. Let go!'

'Hope, what the fu–?'

The atmosphere has changed: it's uncomfortable when normally it's happy. Protesters are looking at me in disbelief. What have I done? What's wrong?

He's pointing at my hand. There is a sign there, a girl drew it on at school. I don't know what it means. My words are tumbling out, and there are tears running down my face.

'What?'

'Hope – that!'

He points at the drawing on my hand.

'What?'

'What, you really don't know?'

'No!'

My voice is getting smaller and smaller. I am shaking. Nelson on his column is looking down on me. The pigeons are crapping all over Nelson's hat and I kinda know how he feels.

The protester relaxes his grip.

'OK, Hope, if you wash that off, you can stay.'

I run to the fountain in the middle of the square and scrub, scrub, scrub until I am sure I can't see it any more. I've no idea what the sign means: it's just two straight lines crisscrossed, bent different ways at each end. I walk slowly back to the group whose home is under Nelson and who are fighting for another Nelson. Whatever it is, that symbol almost lost me my protester friends. I decide I hate the symbol.

For years those guys stayed in front of South Africa House; for years they stood as a symbol of the hope for a free South

Africa. Apart from that one incident, they showed me nothing but kindness. They looked out for me as I wandered the square, letting me collect funds for their cause.

I now realize the significance of a swastika drawn on the hand of a white girl at the Nelson Mandela protest, and feel proud that the protesters stuck to their principles and made me wash it off. Years later, when I told my social worker this story, it was met with a sigh.

'Is that all, Hope? If only I'd known where you were, if only we had known ... We wouldn't have worried so much, wouldn't have thought you were out repeating your mother's behaviour.'

I don't know what shocks me more, the fact that he thought I was becoming my mother when really I was with the protesters, or that he was worried about me.

Running away, 1987

Debbie and I are outside my mum and dad's house. We've run away from Chesterfields together this time. We're bored, and we haven't managed to steal any aerosols, so figured Mum and Dad would get us some booze. I never really enjoy coming here, but I do miss them, especially me dad. I get confused sometimes, like I really, really want to see them, but they've never really wanted me around, and they do such crappy stuff to me, it makes me feel bad. Debbie says it's humiliating, but she is a little bit older than me and ever so pretty, so she understands what humiliation means better than me. She explains that it's when adults do stuff to make you feel really bad. She knows as she has also had a really bad time, although her bad time was different from mine.

She was taken into care permanently when her mum went to prison and 'cos there was no one around to look after her, not that they ever did. She didn't go home when her mum came out of prison, so she's stayed in lots of homes. She says that in the homes where she's been in Hackney, the care workers do lots of horrid things like touching the older girls and even the boys. I've noticed that all the girls who've come from other homes speak about it. They say it's normal in many of the homes. They like Chesterfields 'cos it's different.

Thank fuck I've never had to deal with that.

We still run away, though; whenever something happens that makes the world feel like it's on its head, we go. We've just been to her mum's flat, but she wouldn't let us stay over. Her mum says it's 'cos it'll look bad to the social worker, when she's trying to fight in the courts to get Debbie back. Debbie says it's 'cos she's a selfish cow and she bets her mum's boyfriend is coming round. Debbie said it was boring there anyhow, so we left. To be helpful, I said Mum and Dad would let us stay, as they don't give a crap about the social workers, or getting us home. Now we're here, I'm not so sure.

The door, as always, is on the latch, so we push it open. My parents are in the kitchen, drunk already, with a new man I've not seen before. Dad introduces him as 'Judge' and goes off to get some more spirits from the shop.

'Replenishments coming up, all free, of course!' he jokes.

The room becomes a little bit spinny. I am used to booze, but today I feel a little unsteady. I don't think we've eaten all day. When I see the Judge moving closer to my mum, I know it's time for Debbie and me to leave. I announce, 'Right, time to go, I've got school tomorrow.'

They laugh, and send me on my way. As I leave, the Judge puts his dirty fuckin' hand down my mum's blouse and Dad shows us the door.

'What, wha', where am I? Debbie?'

She's gone, I've no idea where. I'm on the top deck of a bus, and the driver is standing over me.

'Get off me, you dirty old fuck.'

'I'm not touching ya. You've been sick on the bus and then fell asleep, you little tyke.'

I look around me: everything is covered in yellow goo. I grab my throat, which is burning and tastes of whisky. My body feels like shite, and involuntarily I convulse and puke again, narrowly missing the bus driver, but covering more of his precious bus.

The coppers are here now too.

Cheeky, be cheeky.

'Oh what a nice surprise to see you, officer . . .'

'What's your name, dear?'

'Dear, my name isn't dear. I salute the officers of the law for their fuckin' intelligence.' Hand up, affect the salute.

Ha ha I am sooo funny.

'All right then, but you have to tell me your name, and where you are from.'

'My name is my business, although I will divulge to you officers of the law in my bestest London, that I am from this 'ere borough of Camden.'

He he, I'm brilliant, they will like that.

They don't like that.

'This isn't Camden, young lady.'

'Oooh, where is it then?'

My finger points out, in front of my eyes, towards the copper, and I follow it as it draws a circle in the air. My body follows my finger, swaying in a circle. I giggle. This is fun.

'Peckham.'

'What? Where? How? Fuck!'

Not so much fun now is it, Hope?

The more I swear, the angrier they get; the less I tell them, the angrier they get; the more I think I am funny – *this is just brilliant.*

Whatever I do, the less humour they seem to see, and the funnier I think I am, until a thought appears:

I may be pissed, ha ha . . . but hold on . . . I'm in Peckham, how the fuck? I don't remember a thing. Sober, be sober, Hope. Think. Think.

Eventually I tell them: 'Hope, my name's Hope. I'm from Chesterfields Children's Home in North London.'

'All right. All right, Hope.' The copper's voice is kind, calm, relieved. 'Now why didn't you just tell us that before?'

'Well I thought I was in Camden, not fuckin' Peckham.' I pause, I smile and continue, 'I didn't know until now that I needed you to give me a lift home, officer. Hic!'

Discovered, 1987

'Hope, what's this?'

'Dunno, white deodorant on a towel, Betty.'

'Hope, are you sniffing aerosols?'

'No, Betty, how can you say such a thing? I would'na do that . . .'

'You must stop. It will damage your brain. If it carries on, Hope, we shall have to send you somewhere else.'

But it makes me feel good. It helps me escape the feeling of hating myself. You just want to send me away, you old witch.

Notes, taken by Hope, in 1993, from social services files:

Extract from police report, 23 October 1987

— 1.30 a.m. police called to Children's Home – met by a senior social worker.

— Apparently Hope Daniels and another girl, Debbie Smith, locked themselves in one of the rooms at the home.

— Phoned their boyfriends in Iceland & caused damage to the room by smashing a picture, plant pots and taking the telephone socket out of the wall.

— Both arrested.

— Another social worker came to the station and withdrew the allegation.

— Daniels and Smith were given into the care of their social workers and returned to the home.

Erica's house, 1987

Since the incident at the home, my mate Erica's mum, Alice, has been really kind to me. She lets me come round to their house more often after school, and I even get to stay over. The social worker had to ask the judge in the courthouse, and he said it was OK. I'm spending Christmas with them. On the one hand, that is really, really exciting. On the other, it's really annoying. Since the mess-up of the office, where we read the log book and called Gary, who was in Iceland on a school trip, my pocket money has been cut as a punishment. I've no money for presents. I don't want to steal anything 'cos then it's not the same and Erica's mum might stop me seeing them.

Can't risk it.

I know, I know, I know.

I am bouncing up and down with excitement. I have bags of energy, now I have finally solved the problem that's been worrying me for days. *How do I get decent presents for Erica's family to give to them at Christmas? Now I know I am a genius. I have a great plan.*

I look at my Christmas list – the list of presents Chesterfields will get me. Betty looks at it and raises an eyebrow.

'Do you really want a book about volcanoes and a Meccano set, Hope?'

I nod furiously, biting my bottom lip. Hoping my lie won't be found out. This is important to me.

Waiting for Christmas, I can feel the pressure in my head. What if I get caught?

The usual increased noise level on Christmas morning. The others tear open their presents. I carefully remove the Sellotape from mine.

Don't rip the paper, careful. Careful.

I manage to open them all, and I don't even have to fake that I love everything I've got. I scoop them all up, run up the stairs, and wrap them all back up. The Sellotape doesn't quite stick, but that's OK. I place each one carefully in my bag.

I have presents!

Erica and her family love everything I've managed to get for them. Roger likes his volcano book, and Steve loves the Meccano. I feel welcome. I catch Erica's mum in the kitchen, cooking turkey. I run over and give her a hug.

'I just wanted to say thanks for all you have done for me.'

'That's all right, love, we like having you here. You are a good girl, just had a few bad breaks. Nothing we can't work through, eh!'

'I've had the best day.'

'It's a long way from being over, love. Now, get out of my hair while I finish lunch.'

The best bit of the day turned out not to be when Roger gave me and Erica the same present – a Walkman each – even though that was pretty good. The best bit of the day, of the week, of the year, was when he ruffled my hair and called me his sister.

I remember listening to Bros on my Walkman, and that feeling of being part of a proper family at last – it was like floating high and higher than the clouds, and for that feeling I am eternally grateful.

New Year's Eve, 1987

'My 'ead hurts.'

'So does mine,' says Erica.

'Yer mum was OK last night, wasn't she?'

'Yeah. Oh my God, we were so drunk! I thought she'd go mad. What we doin' tonight then, Hope?'

'Trafalgar Square. Me mates have a car.'

We go downstairs. Erica's mum has laid out a whole big breakfast of eggs and all the things we can't face.

'How are you feeling, girls?'

'OK, thanks.'

'Hmmm. What are you up to tonight?'

'Off to Trafalgar Square. Me mates have a car. They can take us, the Brosettes, up to town and we can Par–r–ty!'

Erica's mum stops. Sits down.

'Girls, I would prefer if you stay home tonight. Drinking and going out at your age worries me. I really worry about you both when you go out. Trafalgar Square is a dangerous place for young girls. I would prefer if you decided not to go.'

Someone is treating me like an adult, asking me not to go out, to stay in and be safe with her. I look at Erica. She looks at me. We decide there and then to spend New Year's Eve at home.

We watch Trafalgar Square on the telly. We laugh. We drink Fanta and it feels safe and warm. We discuss them looking into fostering me on a permanent basis. My own happy family.

16

SPECIAL BREW

Running, 1988

Betty says Erica's family can't foster me 'cos she's a single mum, and that no one suitable has replied to my advert. But my fostering social worker told me lots of people replied, I know they did. I lie on my bed, looking at the ceiling.

You are a liar. A liar, Betty. But maybe it's the fostering social worker tellin' me what she thinks I wanna hear. Maybe she is the liar. You can't trust adults.

I feel the need to run away.

'Shit.'

Oh no. Oh no. Oh no. Is he still following me? Are they all watching me? Yes. Walk away, slowly. I'm not scared, I'm not. I'm not. I am. I am. Smelly man. Why did they want me to kiss him? They think I'm like Mum. Walk tall. I can't breathe. Don't cry.

Footsteps. Running behind me. Shit. The man. I turn round, putting all my energy into:

'FUCK OFF!'

Thud. My face is on the ground.

Lie still, Hope, still.

'Fuckin' bitch.'

Footsteps walking away.

I lie on the ground, in the dirt, unable to breathe. I hear the traffic towards Camden Road at the edge of the park. I pick myself up, my face throbbing, and I run.

They think I'm like Mum. I am like Mum, putting myself in a situation like that. Why did he want to kiss me? Dirty old fucker.

I run. I run. I stop only when I know I am far away from the guys who pretended to be my friends. They didn't want me really, they didn't like me really. No one likes me; they only have me around because I am like my mum. Why did he want to kiss me? I don't fancy him. He's so old. Smells too. My body convulses, I can't stop it. I need to be sick. Leaning over a wall, I'm sick into someone's back garden. A nice present for them in the morning. Still I retch until there is nothing left. My body stops fighting and I realize I'm alone. Exhausted, I turn to sit on the wall. Legs swinging as people pass by, I look at them coldly.

I can't remember where I've been, what I've been doing. I'm getting a bit sick of all the Tennent's and Special Brew. I'm in a shop, about to lift some more, along with a couple of aerosols. I notice the date on the newspapers. I've been away from the home for four days now.

Fuck. Fuck. 12th March. What have I done the last four days? Fuck.

I know. I was in some guy's flat.

Was I? Fuck. Fuck.

I lift the cans and, without paying, leave.

Were the police there, at the flat? Looking for me? It's a haze. Men moving in and out, telling me it's OK. Feeding me pills.

I called Erica and she says she will come and collect me in the morning. I'm on Hampstead Heath. I am really scared now.

Sit down here, on a bench. It's freezing. Where am I? Ah, that's right. I am on the heath. Fuck, it's dark. That's right. Sleepyhead.

I wake up lying on the ground. My face is damp. It's not just the grass that's wet: my face is sticky and my hair matted. I pull my hair across my face and smell it.

Oh for fuck's sake, not again.

I rub at my hair, trying to remove the sick. I stand up.

Where am I? Must get back to Chesterfields. Oops. Careful.

I stumble and fall head first into a bush.

I am on a bench, next to the tennis courts on Hampstead Heath. Someone has just woken me up.

Erica?

Not Erica. An old man, he's older than my dad. He has a dog. It's dark still.

'What are you doing here? You should come back to my house, it's safe there.'

'No, it's OK, I uh . . . I'll come if your wife says it's OK.'

'OK, OK.'

He leaves.

Whew. Scary old fucker. Dirty bugger.

He's back. He shakes me awake again. I am so out of it, he is now two dirty ol' fuckers, both talking at the same time.

'You must come, my house is OK, it's safe. I've asked my wife, she says you should come.'

He is holding out his hand to me. I look at it.

Shit, what should I do? Mummy, I'm scared, what should I do? Erica is going to come and get me, but not until morning. It's still really dark, and I'm still pissed. What shall I do?

I scratch my head. There is a look in his eye.

Run, Hope, run.

That is what I do. Banging into things, falling over.

Don't look behind you. Don't look behind. Get off the Heath. What's an old man like that doing on the Heath at this time of night? Fuck. The wall hits me again and again as I stumble and fall up Highgate West Hill towards the place I most want to be in the world. Home. I'm cold. I'm pissed.

I will be better, I will be. I don't want to be scared any more. Help me please.

Images spring to mind of Strawberry Shortcake duvets, laughter, food, cuddles and hot chocolate, a place of safety and adults I can trust; people who want me as their sister. Through the haze of each drunken trip of a thirteen-year-old, I see for the first time what people are trying to do for me, and a thought dawns:

I am very lucky.

I am home at last. Betty is there. She looks really sad, and scared. I'm confused, 'cos even though I stink, she hugs me.

'Hope, we have been so worried. We've had the police searching for you for days.'

'Yeah right, who cares? You don't.'

'Enough, Hope. That's it. Enough. I am at my wits' end with you. Go and have a shower. Then we shall talk. I am calling your social worker to say we've found you. Christ, Hope. I'm not sure what else we can do for you.'

Midrange Lodge, 1988

My new key worker, Martha, has taken me out for tea, at McDonald's!

Excellent. Maybe I shall tell her about my need to drink and run away. I want to be able to control what I do. Maybe she will help me.

My Big Mac is in front of me. I'll just have a couple of bites and then tell her I'm fed up with running and want to stop.

Martha speaks first:

'Hope, you won't be going home to Chesterfields this evening, or tomorrow.' She pauses, looks at me with a lowered head, and when I don't answer she carries on nervously. 'I am going to take you to a place which will try and help you work out why you are so unhappy. I have a holdall in the car with a few of your things, some clothes and books that I have packed for you. It's a place that can help you, Hope.'

I say nothing, because too many thoughts are raging through my head.

What! But you didn't warn me of anything. I didn't get to say goodbye to my brothers. What, don't they want me at Chesterfields? They can't want me. How dare you take me away from them? But then if I'm going they don't want me. Oh no, again and again people don't want me around. I'm not wanted at Chesterfields and you tricked me out of the house, and you tell me in a public place so I won't kick off. What are you people? It's not fair. Be strong, Hope, be strong. Don't tell them nothing.

Put on the hard face. Trust no one. There is no one to trust. Bastards. Bastards.

I look up at Martha. I can see she is waiting for me to create a scene, ready for it. Instead, I change my face so it's expressionless and carry on eating my burger.

I look at the sign on the front gate: 'Midrange Lodge'. There is no colour to the place, and so the name fits. It looks drab and like it could do with a lick of paint. High wire fences round it. Big grey door.

It looks like a prison. Horrid. Horrid. Horrid.

'What kind of place is this?' I ask, but am ignored by Martha. In a deadpan, strong voice, I try again: 'Martha, you have to tell me what's going on, it's my life. Tell me!'

Still she doesn't answer, but this time her face cracks and she looks at me sadly.

Is that a tear in her eye? Is she upset? Am I being set up? How? How?

It sounds like the door is being unlocked from the inside. When the staff member lets us in, she locks it behind us. Every door we go though, and there are three, she opens with a key hanging from a chain. There are a lot of keys on that chain. We walk through and she locks the doors behind us.

I am locked in! Fuck. They are locking me in.

'Why are you locking me in?'

Silence in response.

'For fuck's sake, why are you locking me in?'

Nothing. I am met with silence and locked doors.

I feel trapped, caged, and the need to react, to escape, to take control of my own life, arrives like a tornado.

How dare they lock me up? I've not done anything wrong. I am thirteen!

'What the fuck are you doing, locking me up?' I am kicking, screaming, punching the doors. Crying hysterically. I know it's me, but it feels like someone else. This is happening to someone else. But it's not, it's happening to me.

'Martha, please leave, we can handle this.'

'No! No! No! I want Martha. I don't know you. Who the fuck are you, why are you locking me up?'

The restraints are on before I notice, and before Martha has left the room. She looks like she's been punched in the tummy, ashen white to my red tear-stained, angry face. I'm bundled into a room. I'm so angry and scared I hardly hear them telling me to, 'Calm down. We can't reason with you if you're like this. Calm down.'

Still they won't tell me why I am here. The door shuts behind me. I spin round, banging and banging, hoping someone will rescue me. There is a hatch on the door which opens from the outside.

'Calm down and we'll let you out.' As the hatch shuts, I hear someone sigh. 'Solitary is the best place for her.'

I turn round. The whole room, the floor, the ceiling and the walls, are padded. Empty apart from beanbags. The walls are cushioned.

What's going on? What are they doing to me? Why won't anyone tell me? Why won't anyone speak to me?

I sink into a beanbag, exhausted from my screaming and fighting back, and cry.

I hear the key in the lock, and the door opens. I know my face is red with crying, but I don't care. I'm so tired I can be nothing other than calm. The staff take me through endless locked doors and yellow corridors to what they call a 'unit' at the top of the building.

They leave me standing there in what looks like a communal games area, with other, much older girls sitting around looking bored. They don't introduce me to the girls, so I know it's not like Chesterfields. It definitely feels weird; it really doesn't feel as nice.

Immediately the staff leave, the much older girls surround me.

'What you in for, then?'

I can't answer, as I don't know myself I am so confused.

'What . . . you don't know that? Where you from?'

'Chesterfields.'

This girl, who towers above me, immediately asks, 'Do you know a girl called Debbie? She lives there.'

Five girls surround me, all looking at me like they want to kill me. I take the line of least resistance.

Careful, Hope, you don't want to piss these girls off.

'Yeah, I know her.'

Fuck.

The girl who asked me if I know Debbie immediately lunges forward to attack me. The other girls are egging her on. An alarm goes somewhere, and – just as she is about to thump me with a 'Fucking bitch, give her this from me!' – the staff run in, grab her arm and pull me away. The other girls are fighting each other, but I'm not sure why. It's chaos. I'm removed and put back in the padded room for no reason.

Shit, not a good start.

* * *

It's dark outside now. About an hour ago, the staff showed me my room, and gave me a set of pyjamas and a toothbrush.

'Where is my bag? Martha packed me a bag?'

'There is no bag, Hope, we didn't get a bag. You arrived in what you are wearing.'

The room is long and thin. Grey. No colour. It's like a medical ward, only there's a lock on the door. It's not locked now, and one of the girls comes into my room. She had been allowed out that day, so she wasn't here when I arrived, and she wasn't one of the girls who tried to attack me. We exchange names. Her name is Abby and she has a shaved head.

'How come you are allowed out?' I ask.

'I will share a spliff with you if you tell me about Debbie.'

'I don't know what you want to know . . .'

'Who's she seeing?'

'Oh, a guy called Mark.'

'That boy, right, Mark – the big girl who tried to attack you, she's seein' the same man. That's why they attacked you. A tip, little un, don't tell nobody nothin', OK?'

'OK.'

'Good, stick wi' me and I will learn you the ropes. What the fuck you doin' inside anyhow? You gotta be what, twelve, thirteen?'

'Thirteen.'

'Fuck, they lock 'em up young these days.'

'How old are you?'

'Sixteen, almost seventeen. Most of the girls 'ere are.'

'Oh.'

After that, I can't sleep.

I don't know what to do. Those other girls really scare me. But how dare they lock me up? What the fuck is going on?

In the morning, the doors are all unlocked at once, and I'm shown where the dining room is. I'm met with vicious looks and girls gnashing their teeth together at me as I pass. The atmosphere is tense. They are going to hit me . . . Careful, Hope, watch out for it. I look at the staff. They don't seem to give a shit and don't react at all to the teeth baring. They just carry on as if nothing is happening.

I hate all of you, staff and girls. I hate you. I hate you. I gotta work out how to get out of here. They have told me nothin' except I am going to be assessed for a month. Assessed for fuckin' what?

I'm walking down the corridor, back to my room, when I spot it. A fire alarm glass box! I smile for the first time in days. Ha-ha. I've set fire alarms off before for fun, at school and at Chesterfields.

We will all have to go outside if the alarm goes off.

I spend the rest of the day planning when the best time is to set it off. I wait until teatime, thinking that at that time the staff will be busy and not think too much about why the alarm is going off.

I leave my room, walk along the corridor, turn, look at it straight on, and smash the glass over the box.

Wha! Wha! Wha! The alarm shrills through the building. The staff are running around, shouting. 'Come on everyone, down the stairs.'

I'm shaking with fear and adrenaline. I hold on to my hands, so they don't give me away.

I'm going, this is it.

The doors are all open, with the keys on a chain. We are

all led outside, and as soon as the evening sun hits my face, I'm free. I'm out.

I run as fast as I can, all the way down Ostrich Road. Thump, thump. My heart is thumping like nothing I have ever felt. My heart is so loud I think it will burst out of my chest.

I hope I don't have a heart attack.

I find a phone box and ring Phillip.

'Phillip, I am on the Ostrich Road, at the bottom. I am behind the McDonald's. Come and meet me. Now, Phillip, it's urgent. Now. OK, thanks, see you soon. I will wait. Yes, behind McDonald's. Phillip. Don't tell anyone you is comin'.'

Phillip takes me back to Chesterfields, where Harold and Jack hide me in the basement. The first time they bring me food, I see the staff behind them.

'I hate Midrange Lodge. They bully me. It would be better if you let me come home. I will be good, I will. I promise. I won't run away. I want to stay.'

My heart feels like it's being pulled out. I want to be at home. Chesterfields is my home. Why are they pushing me out?

'You have to go back, Hope, there is a court order. We will take you, make sure you are OK.'

I lower my head.

Think, think.

'OK, if I have to. I just need to go to the bathroom first.' As soon as I leave the room, I dart out of the front door, jumping on the first bus that will take me to freedom. I have no money, but I know how to avoid the conductor – it's a game I've played for years.

I walk and walk around the West End, thinking how much I hate myself and everyone else.

They can go fuck themselves. I don't fuckin' care.

I truly didn't care what happened to me.

I am back now, in the kitchen at Chesterfields. I'm starving. I was on the run for four days. I ran out of mates to stay with, and had a close shave when my social worker was standing outside school when I went to meet Erica. She told me I had to come home.

I'm looking at the cheese and pickle sandwich they've made me, wanting to eat it so quickly but enjoying the flavour, when police walk into the kitchen.

A mouthful of sandwich is sprayed across the table as I swear. 'Shit.' I finish my mouthful and let rip:

'What you go and tell the coppers for? I don't want to go back there. I hate you. I want to stay here. I don't want to go there. I don't want to be locked up. I'm thirteen. All the other girls are sixteen. Why am I there? Why can't I be here? I hate you.'

The police, as ever, are very kind to me. They take me off in their car but don't lock me up. The police station looks a little different from Stokie Nick. But it's the same colour, and even has the same posters: 'Stop Crime!' They let me sit in a room where they solve all the crimes. I'm happy they're keeping me out of the cells. There is this one policewoman who speaks to me like an adult. I've seen her before, but this is the first time we've spoken.

For some reason, I trust her and tell her all about Midrange Lodge. They call the staff from Midrange in front of me.

Oh no, they don't believe me.

But they do. I listen as the policewoman's boss, the chief inspector, really has a go at them for not keeping me safe. I giggle. He frowns nicely and tells me to shhh. I smile, and my back straightens so I sit up straight.

He tells them that the WPC is bringing me back with him, and they both want to have a look round. He smiles at me.

Ohhhh. On hearing this, I start crying really hard. The police try and make me smile, but they can't hide from me – someone who knows – that behind the smiles, I can see they all just look really sad.

When the police take me back, a big man with a kind face meets us. He takes us all into his office.

'Hope,' he said firmly, 'we are very sorry for what you experienced here. I have spoken to everyone and it will all be OK now.' I stare at him with my hardest stare, unable to get the words out.

I don't believe you, man with no name. Why didn't you tell me your name, is it 'cos you is lying to me?

I look to the police officer: 'Please, please don't leave me here. Please take me back to Chesterfields. I don't belong here. I'm too young.'

The policewoman with the nice face and voice speaks: 'They can't take you back, Hope. There is a court order for you to stay here.'

I hear the words she speaks differently from what she says. I hear: 'They can't take you back 'cos Chesterfields don't want you.'

In my head, it's so clear.

I'm left there in the office. The police leave and I'm taken back upstairs. I wait an hour. I'm so bored just sitting. Then I think:

Fuck it.

I run down the hall and, screaming with delight, I set the fire alarm off again. This time the staff are ready for me, but we all still have to be taken outside. It's the rules. Once we're outside, I try and do another runner. I get to the top of the road, but the staff are waiting to take me back.

I'm back in the man with no name's office. He looks very stern.

I don't give a shit what you say, mister no name.

'Hope, we cannot guarantee your safety. I am going to place you in solitary confinement, and there you will wait for your social worker. She will be here tomorrow.'

Another night of not sleeping.

What will they do to me? Why can't anyone tell me why I'm here? What have I done? Why does no one want me?

In the morning I walk into the office, chewing on my bottom lip. I'm in trouble now. Both my social worker and my senior social worker have turned up. I look at the clock. It's not even 7.30 a.m.

'Hope, we are moving you to another secure unit, Calakow House, near Croydon.' My shoulders slump, but I say nothing. I am tired, I am confused. I feel beaten. 'I don't care any longer, do what you have to do.'

And then, a strange thing. My lady social worker hugs me, right in the office in front of the man with no name, and her boss. She stands there, hugging me. 'It's all going to be OK.'

Notes, taken by Hope, in 1993, from social services files:

Date: 25 March 1988, 08.30. Hope Daniels
In accordance with Secure Accommodation Regulations 1983, the above named girl was admitted to Secure Accommodation in Calakow House on the date and time recorded above.

Placed in Secure as a result of 'chronic absconding'.

17

SECURE

Calakow House, 1988

How do I get out of here? There are so many doors. It smells of cleaning fluid. I went through five doors to get in here, all clanged shut behind me. But at least they are nicer to me here.

We are upstairs in this building: the open unit is below us. The superintendent and her huge bunch of keys met me, at the end of the corridor of doors.

'There is no way out and don't try the fire alarm route, Hope, or you will be banned from playing tennis.'

Fuck, they know.

I tried each door. They were all locked.

One of the girls who has been here for six months found me. 'There is no way out, yeah, we've all tried. You get through one door and then there's another one. All locked, all over the place.'

I will find a way to get out by tomorrow. Who needs a stupid assessment anyway? I want to go and see my mates, I need a drink. I need to not feel trapped, controlled, to lose myself for a bit. Think, think.

I bang my head with the palm of my hand, as if that will help.

At dinner time, we all sit down to eat our meal at long tables. Just like in the TV programme *Porridge*! It's like the last place, and yet it's not like the last place. The girls here are nicer, and the staff seem to care.

The girl who spoke to me earlier is sitting next to me. She's called Fiona. She is really, really skinny. She doesn't like food. She asks me:

'Here, do you want this? I'll give you a fag if you take it.'

She scrapes some food off her plate onto mine. I watch as she pretends to eat until the staff turn away, then whoosh, there is a little less food on her plate, and a bit more on mine. The smell of shepherd's pie escapes as she cuts it up.

'It's disgusting!' she says.

'Fantastic,' is my response.

Fags and extra food. Great!

'God! Why can't you give me some booze?'

'Hope, you are thirteen.'

'Yeah, but I'm locked up for no fuckin' reason.'

'They want to assess you.'

'Yeah, and they're doin' my head in. I want a drink.'

'You can't have one.'

'Why the fuck not?'

'You are thirteen.'

'OK, give me an aerosol.'

'You know we can't do that. Look, give me a second, sit down.'

I do as I'm told.

'Hope, we're worried for you. You have a bright future. It's only a few weeks in here. I, all the staff, really care about you. You're a bright happy child. But you are a child. Let us look out for you, eh? We know what's best. It isn't drink. You'll end up hurting yourself if you carry on like this.'

'I don't care. No one likes me. No family wants me. No one has chosen me. What's the point?'

My head is in my hands.

'You're worth more than you're giving yourself credit for. You have to be careful, or you will end up like your mother.'

'What? Ah fuck off!' I run out.

I need to get out of here. Now.

I can't breathe, I feel trapped, like my breath is all swollen inside of me. Never, never will I be like her.

I hate her. Hope, you gotta do what you can to not be like her. I have to get out of here. How? How? How? Think . . . I need a drink so bad.

I am marching up and down, wringing my hands.

Think! The only way I will get a drink is to get out of here. Oh my God! Ha-ha! I've got it! What a brilliant idea! Why didn't I think of it before – the food lift! It goes down to the kitchens that are in the open unit. The girls downstairs will help me. I know some of them from Chesterfields. Brilliant! I can go in the lift after lunch. Fiona said the cooks all knock off at half past two.

I'm so excited at lunch I feel like I have ants crawling all around my pants. I'm so looking forward to the prospect of being outside, free, able to have a drink, to lose myself for a bit, that I'm almost unable to eat my double portions of lunch. I tell no one.

It doesn't take me long to get into the lift. I pull the doors down, and curl up like a foetus inside its mother's womb. It's tight and I'm ready to move now. Crap! I haven't told anyone my plan. So there is no one to press the button for it to go up and down. I try to manoeuvre myself out.

Ow! Shit I'm stuck.

I can't open the door as my arm is wedged against it. I sit in the lift waiting for someone to press the button.

Everyone is playing tennis and I'm stuck in here. Pisser. Fuck, ow that's sore.

Cramp has come in to join me. My left foot tightens. Oh bloody hell that's all I need. I start laughing. I hear someone and bang on the door of the lift. Whoever it is hears me. My heart pounds, but I want out of the lift more than I am bothered about being in real trouble. Whoever it is is opening the hatch.

Whew!

'Fiona!'

'What are you doing in there?'

'Escaping. Go on, press the button to push the lift down.'

'The only button is downstairs, and you'll never get the staff to help ya. It's all controlled from down there.'

'Oh. Shit. Right, OK then, I will have to have another think. Ow! I've got cramp. Can you help me out then?'

She pulls an arm, then a leg. We are both laughing as I'm extracted from the lift in an ungainly manner. Fiona is so skinny she isn't able to balance me, so I slump out into a heap on the floor, still giggling. I look at the clock on the wall. Two hours I've spent in that lift waiting to get out. If I had stayed where I was meant to, I could have been playing tennis.

Review, 1988

I am to be put under the spotlight, undertake a review.

A review of what? They got me bloody files: they should know what's in them. I don't and it's not fair. Can't wait till I'm old enough to get my hands on those files.

The woman doctor is looking at me funny. They all do. This is the fifth one I've seen in as many days. I'm knackered. They won't leave me alone. They look at me and speak in a really soft voice, not like their normal voice that they use on other people. But really soft and slow, like I can't understand what's going on. They look at me like I'm a curiosity. *I'm a person not a thing.* The girls told me the doctors will ask me all sorts of questions, like what do I think of this, what do I think of that? The doctors are obsessed with whether or not someone has fiddled with you and the effects of this and that. I decided I would play them, but now, apart from the tone of their voices, the psychiatrists and psychologists start saying stuff that makes some sense, and so I've started to tell them what's going on in my head.

I'm a bit scared at first, to speak about this stuff. They give me some toys and a folder of puzzles that helps me to get the words out. When they first gave me this stuff, I hated it. I spat out: 'What the fuck are you giving me this shit for? I hate being assessed. I hate you. I hate everyone, I hate everything. Why can't you leave me alone so I can have a drink?'

'We can't do that, Hope.'

They were patient with me. Helped me calm down. Suddenly, it pops out my mouth. I'm tired. I want these feelings of confusion to stop. The words just pop out and, now they have, I can't take them back. Can't put them back inside me. They are there floating around in the air between the psychotherapist and me.

'I hate my mother's profession. She is shameful.'

This is the first time I am really able to speak about the stuff that went on and how I feel about it. Not having this stuff stuck in my head makes me feel a bit better. These people are listening to me; they don't react badly to what I tell them. So I carry on:

'I'm really worried I'm going to become an addict, like my mum. I can become obsessed with things and people.'

'Can you help me understand that a bit more, Hope?'

'Well, it's like running away, or my files. Every day, I think, what is in my files? What are they writing in the log book? I can't get to them, so it feels like the pressure is building in my head, in my chest, so I will burst. I can't cope with the pressure, unless I have a fag or a drink. I don't understand how I can't get words out to tell people I'm hurting, and so I run away. I feel this need to run, run, run and there is nothing I can do to stop it.'

She nods, she looks kindly, and she gives me reassurance, enough that I carry on. Now I'm talking it's difficult to stop me.

'I feel worn out by life. It's just crap.'

'And what is it like being here, Hope?'

'What, the secure unit?'

'Yes.'

'It's great.'

She raises her left eyebrow. 'Really?'

'In here, like, you don't have to think for yourself, 'cos you aren't even allowed to wear shoes. I never have to make a decision about anything. It's safe here, there is food here, served at set times. There is no pressure. No one expects me to go and see my parents.'

That reminds me to ask about my mum and dad. I am so curious about what my parents say about me to these professionals, I could burst.

'Can I ask you something?'

'Of course you can, Hope.'

It tumbles out: 'What did my parents say about me? Were they drinking when you met them?'

'Well, they were worried about you, and yes, they had been drinking, so we couldn't really interview them.'

Each professional tells me the same, and each time the shame at their behaviour comes flooding back to me, like an old unwanted friend. Mixed with a small voice in the back of my head telling me that this is what I will turn into.

'I want to be different to my parents. Do you think I can be?'

'Yes, Hope, I do. You are a clever girl, with real determination and resourcefulness. With the right support, and if we make sure you don't have so much responsibility for someone so young, yes, I think you will do OK.'

'It's hard, you know, I ain't stupid, but everyone at school, they could see I was rotten, they all knew about my mum, told me that I would grow up just like her.' I'm fiddling with my jeans. 'Do you think I'm stupid? What you gonna write in that report?'

She smiles. 'Now, Hope, you know I can't tell you that.'

'But they are my files, it's about me . . . Why can't I know what you write, what's in them? They are mine, mine, mine. About me! Why can't I know what you say about me?'

The lack of information means my obsession over these files is constantly being fed.

Notes, taken by Hope, in 1993, from social services files:
Interviews with Hope (me) and educational psychologist: April 20th and 28th, and April 25th and May 4th 1988

— Hope – co-operative in interviews. Mature for age, gave appropriate sense of importance to the difficult issues discussed.

— Staff changes at Chesterfields – happened at a crucial stage in life – proved to be disturbing. Perception is that younger brothers were happy at Chesterfields, whereas Hope's reaction to staff changes was to abscond.

— Attitude towards education – definitely wants to go back to school but not boarding school. Wants to be fostered.

— Abilities: concentration – adequate; results on both verbal and performance – middle of the average range. Reliable and consistent.

— Unsettled circumstances and noting highest sub-score (which is the high average range) on verbal reasoning sub-tests. Results may represent a minimum estimate of potential abilities.

— Dismissed any concern that she might develop an alcohol problem (risk – identifying with parents esp. when there is a distressing break in relationships – the psychologist made a note that she did not mention this to me.)

Why Not?!

— Can talk to staff. Hope would like to try group [therapy] again. Psychologist says this is important to organize – as needs much support and understanding. Teachers can help with reintegrating at school, arrangements for her care and therapeutic approach will be of basic importance in her personal and social adjustment.

Fuck, why did this never happen?

— Hope is close to her brothers – but very distressed at the changes in staff and disruption – reacted in a damaging way. Her needs should be considered separately from brothers.
— An individual fostering arrangement for her IS one option to consider.

Guardian, 1988

She has brought me a McDonald's, my guardian *ad litum*. She's the person the court has appointed to speak for me at the case conferences about me.

I can't see why I can't go myself.

I like her, she sticks up for me. I know my case conference is coming up, 'cos she keeps asking me lots of questions while I try and eat my Big Mac. It's almost cold, by the time she got it from McDonald's and through all the locked doors, but I appreciate it. There must be something she wants to ask me, or tell me. They always take me for a treat at McDonald's when there is something up.

The familiar choking feeling comes to me every time I see her, not 'cos of her, but because I feel suffocated. Throughout my time in care, even before the secure unit, I felt I couldn't sneeze without permission. I had to ask her for everything and my head races with the unfairness of it all.

Why can't I have friends to stay over without their parents being checked by the police? Why can't I stay with friends without them having the police look at their family?

Here, in secure, it's better, 'cos there are no friends to go and stay with. We don't have to bother about shoes or more than one set of clothes, and when we get locked up at night it feels safe. The rules are the rules, so we know where we stand, and most of all I know I am warm, safe and secure, so it feels like a baby cotton blanket.

People who care visit me. Like, Erica's mum came yesterday. I love it when people visit. It makes me feel special. They bring me presents. Books and sweets. Yesterday, Erica's mum got really pissed off at the way I'm being treated. It started with the number of doors she had to go through to get here. She asked me lots of questions, but she didn't seem to like any of my answers. That confused me. I've never seen her be pissed off before.

Even when we did really rubbish stuff, got drunk and went out all the time, she was calm and just told me she worried about me.

At first I thought she was pissed off at me for getting myself into a situation that got me locked up. I sat and listened to her, trying to quiet my head.

'Why aren't you allowed shoes? This is ridiculous. They searched me before I came in here, you know . . . Ridiculous. What do they think I'm bringing you? What is all this about? You haven't done anything. Why have they locked you up in here? I will get you out of here, Hope. I will fight to get you out.'

She is the first person to worry about me.

I like her. She wants to foster me. She asked me yesterday. I said yes.

When she had gone, I lay on my bed and looked at the ceiling. She was really angry that I've been locked up, but actually, it's OK. It's safe and there are boundaries we know not to cross. We get tennis for an hour a day and can do yoga when we have to calm down. I never have to wear shoes. My head is quieter than it has ever been. The only crap bit is I've lost some of my stuff, but that happens to everyone – we all move so often and without warning. We are more interested in saying bye to people than packing. Something always gets left behind.

'How are you, Hope?' asks my guardian.

Wish I had a pound for every time someone asks me that.

'I'm fine, thanks.'

'How are you getting on? Settled in OK?'

'Yes, I like it here. Much better than the open unit.'

'Really? You like being locked up?'

I pause. She lets me think. No pressure from her – that is one of the reasons I like her. No pressure.

'Yeah. I feel safe and secure here. Safe from my own head. The assessments are getting to me a bit, 'cos I have to explain again and again what happened to me, and that no one has ever tried to touch me up. Again and again I have to tell them, I know it's not happened to me but no one seems to believe me 'cos they keep asking me if an adult has done anything I'm not comfortable with.'

'They have to check, Hope. Now, you were telling me why you like being locked up.'

'So I tell them, the only thing you guys have done that I'm not comfortable with is not getting me fostered.'

We both laugh.

'I will tell them at conference. Now, let's get on with preparing your case.'

The afternoon is almost gone.

'Tell me again about why you like being here.'

'Well, even though they are assessing me all the time, it's like the staff here, well, um, they really listen to me, like they want to find out what is best for me. The staff are like prison staff, with all their massive bunches of keys, and I swear they have eyes in the back of their heads. But they are kind to me. But best of all, I don't have to think about anything. No responsibility. Just me and my shoe-less feet.'

'Hope, I understand why you like the security, but you will be moving from here. It depends what the case conference says, but they can't keep you locked up. You're thirteen, all the other girls are three or four years older than you. It's not healthy for you to be here.'

'I don't care. My head is calmer when I'm in here. I want to stay here.'

She sighs, changes the subject and lets me finish my McDonald's. Then she lets drop the reason she is here, the reason for the Big Mac with extra fries.

'Hope, the case conference is coming up. I have to tell them what you want. Can you tell me?'

'You know what I want. I say it all the time. I want to be fostered. Be part of a real family.'

Notes, taken by Hope, in 1993, from social services files:
Psychiatric reports April–May 1988. Calakow House, secure unit.

Hope may not be aware of some of the details of her parents' history ... caution should be exercised in disclosing the material set out below without careful consideration of the likely effects.

Well I know now ...

Background Info:

Mr Daniels (Dad):

— 64 years old – in care from age 3 'til 16

— at 16 went home. Three younger brothers, all about his age. Dad felt abandoned & neglected.

Oh! Poor Dad, that must've been shit.

— Prison many times – mainly shoplifting.

— Dad says: physically healthy but ulcers. Drinking increased after we are in care. Doesn't get help with stopping drinking. Bored with life.

Mrs Daniels: (Mum)

— 49 years old – youngest of 4 kids

— Her Mum – in an old folks' home. Mum not visited for 2 years.

— Her Dad – Merchant Navy, alcoholic and not around much when Mum was a kid.

— Mum put in care – returned home at the age of 17 years. Had first child at 17 – adopted.

— Met Dad at 25 – he's 15 years older.

— M&D evicted 3 times – now in Hamilton Street, a council house.

—They have never been formally married.

Shit! M&D never married. So why did they stay together?

— Mum – long history of alcohol abuse. Prison for shoplifting
& drunk and disorderly.

— Psychologist notes – Mum previously worked as a prostitute. Mum not admitted to this, but said – Hope exposed
to Mum's sexual activities, though not intentionally.
Clients brought back to house. Mum 'thought I was
asleep'.

— M&D – not drunk at the interview but they smelt of booze,
were subdued, smoked heavily throughout. Polite, co-operative and helpful, but blank & out of touch with needs of
kids (us).

— They don't think they should've stopped drinking – even
though it embarrassed us not even to look after us properly. They thought that we were all doing OK.

Why couldn't you stop drinking for us? Addiction over us?
Why?

— Helpless – were in a cycle of prison and poverty.

— Both had very poor parenting themselves so they never
learnt to be good parents. They did not know how to
parent.

Situation at time of review:

— Me, Harold and Jack – 1983. Wards of Court. Settled well.

— For me: changes of staff and puberty disrupted this. Alcohol
and smoking relaxed me.

— Risk of me repeating the cycle of Mum – running away at
night, I didn't tell them where I went. But always came
back, or brought back.

— Counselling at Calakow House – uncertain about starting this. But stayed in contact with my brothers. Was willing to carry on with therapy but told psychiatrist I would stop if didn't like it.

— Realistic – and I knew Court might decide that community home with education best for me.

— But told her if that happened I'd feel like I was not being listened to – again.

Mental State Examination:

— Hope – well-developed girl, physically and sexually mature, cheerful manner. Good eye contact and very good rapport. Speech unremarkable. No disorder of mood, appetite or sleep disturbance.

— No evidence of psychosis or obsessional symptoms. Fully cognitively intact.

— Focus on parents, particularly their behaviour at interview, and their prison sentences. Ashamed of them. Feels sorry for them. Not angry. Doesn't miss them.

— Disgust at prostitution & the idea of 'selling her body'. Vowed would never be a prostitute.

— Prefer not to see parents unless they wouldn't be drunk.

— Understands why she is placed at Calakow, away from Chesterfields 'cos of changes in staff & feeling unsettled. Afraid might impulsively run away if in open unit.

— V. strong wish to be fostered – realizes that this might be difficult. She hopes that if she were treated kindly and the limits explained to her, that she would be able to respond.

— Denied interest in alcohol or drugs or lighter fuel – not afraid of developing a drinking problem.

— No risk of violence. Her insight is good but partial and not inappropriately immature.

Conclusions:

— Normal physical and developmental history, optimistic about returning to school, wants to be fostered – but knows might be difficult.

— Average intelligence and academic potential (given adequate supervision).

— M&D unable to provide a stable environment – what effect this will have, psychologist didn't know. No sign outwardly of being damaged by seeing Mum working – except a lot of swearing.

— At risk of running away – and not speaking to care staff about the need to run away.

— Hope been told that Hackney actively looking for fostering place – and she should have counselling to work through issues of security and relationships and might help to reduce the risk to re-enact her mother's history, but neither have happened so far.

— Hope is also at considerable risk of developing an alcohol dependency disorder.

— Fostering – psychologist thinks this is a risk!

— Can understand the intensity of Hope's wishes to have a family – to develop closeness and intimacy of caring & supportive parents, as well as the wish to have the missed childhood. Must be clear that the reality of Hope's situation makes this very unlikely.

— Will be painful for Hope to come to terms with the fact that she has not had the childhood she should have had and that she has been badly let down by her own parents.

— Difficult for anybody to face, let alone somebody as vulnerable as she is.

— Part of the current problem — adults who have taken over from her parents have limitations on what they can do to support her — no mention of these limitations.

— Tragic if Hope's birth parents' failure to face the reality of their limitations — and holding out false hope were to be repeated by the professionals' inability to face their own limitations.

— Professional people shouldn't hold out false hopes for Hope's future — should recognise the limitations.

— Essential that the imminent review grasps this nettle if it is going to find a way of helping her.

— Hope is going to find this very difficult — hence need for urgent therapy.

— Until she can see that, if nothing else, professional people know their limitations and can face the pain that stirs up, there can be little hope that she will feel she can truly trust anybody.

18

A DECISION

Case conference, 1988.

It is today. I know it is, because they are taking me to yoga.

What happened in the tests. What happened in the tests? I must have done OK in one of them, 'cos even though they are a year away, I have started studying for my GCSEs already 'cos I want to do well.

The staff here say I'm bright, so it won't take me long to catch up, and I have to work hard to make something of myself. I think I might.

They are holding me in a room, the big room, next to the quiet room. That is where the yoga is. I am jumping around like I have a spring inside me. They've told me to stay in the quiet room all day.

I can't wait till they've finished. I want to be in there. I want to know now.

I peek out through the door to see who's attending my case conference. There are about eight or nine of them. Some I don't know – others I do.

There is that psychologist. Shit, what did I tell her again?

I watch them all pass, all of them looking at me with a small smile, a nod, or a word of reassurance – my social worker, her boss, my guardian *ad litem* and my old teacher. She smiles at me as she passes but doesn't speak.

I hope she comes and sees me after they have done. Shit, what happens if the people who don't know me don't listen to them? Foster care, I want to be fostered. Hear me, hear me.

The door of the conference room closing is a nightmare for me. It clicks and then there is silence.

Oh shit, oh shit, I hope they get me fostered. I want to be fostered so badly. Did I tell them enough at the meetings? Did I pass their tests? They are next door, next door! They are discussing me. Why can't I be in the room? It's not fair.

My ear is on the wall, trying to hear what they're saying, but I can't hear a thing. Yoga for me today means pacing from side to side. I am in the room on my own, walking the eight steps from one wall to the other. To mix it up a bit, I walk from one corner to the other corner. A diagonal line, skewed like my life. My heart pumping in time to my fast steps.

These things happen every six months. We all know when they're coming up. This is my seventh one, but still I'm not used to them. Being kept outside, not knowing, is driving me mental. Every time they discuss me behind closed doors, I feel like I'm trapped, caged, and all the control over my life is taken by the decision-makers next door. Pace, pace, pace, back and forth. Thoughts of what could happen being stretched to either wall and back again.

What happens if they tell me I have to start seeing my mum and dad again? I don't want to. I don't want to.

I have no control over what happens to me, and so I wait and I pace and I think jumbled-up thoughts, until they reappear, all smiling and kind. My old teacher is first out the door.

'It's really good to see you, Hope. How are you?'

'I'm fine, Miss, thanks. What happened in there? It's not fair I can't be in that meeting.'

'You know the process, Hope, and that I can't tell you what we decided, but it's all fine. Your social worker will meet with you later. Now, look at you, all growing up. You're looking healthy, and nice blonde hair. So tell me how you are.'

Notes, taken by Hope, in 1993, from social services files: Calakow Regional Resource Centre, Assessment Summary. Nine people made this decision about me.

— Hope – a pleasant and co-operative girl with some insight into her problems. Confidence & ability in school & is capable of achieving educationally.

— School and Chesterfields Children's Home – both would have her back.

— Lengthy discussion. Agreed that, although Hope has asked to return to Chesterfields, she has made no firm commitment regarding her behaviour. If she were to return, she may well repeat the behaviour that put her into Calakow.

— Hope's request, to be fostered – seriously considered as a viable, long-term prospect and that Hope would benefit from a good parenting experience.

— Brothers – contact important, but not necessary that Hope be placed with them on a full-time basis.

— Hope's individual needs may be best served away from her brothers.

Agreed:

— Care plus therapy – important for personal and social development.

— Education – best met in a small learning group: care, consistency and controls of a home with education on the premises – good for Hope. Plus weekends with her brothers, possibly at Chesterfields.

— If foster placement became a reality the home with education would support the transition, and yet offer long-term intervention if no foster placement.

— Beaufort and Ferring Lodges were identified as possible placements while availability at Beaufort and Ferring Lodges is checked.

— Hope to be transferred to Calakow open unit within days.

Being told, 1988

My social worker, the senior social worker and I are all in a room. The atmosphere is heavy. They have just told me the result of the review board. I cannot speak. I just look at the coffee stain on the carpet.

'Crap! It's just crap. What do you mean, a community home with education? I thought you were going to give me what I asked the guardian *ad litem* for – foster carers?'

Why does no one want me? The court must be telling them bad things about me. No one wants me 'cos everyone hates me. Gutted.

Grandma, 1988

There is another door in front of me that I don't want to go through. This time it's a cheap brown door that has a big spring to make it swing shut by itself. There's a window in the door with the fire wire through it, like every place I have stayed since I left home. I focus past the wire, where an old lady, with shoulders so curved her neck is sticking out at right angles to her spine, is sitting in a chair being fed by a nurse. Mushy brown food that is being slid from a blue plastic bowl via a blue plastic spoon into the old lady's mouth and from there onto her chin.

The old lady doesn't look like my grandma but I am told it is. She asked to see me. I push the door: it is heavier than it looks, holding me back another second from saying hello to this woman who no longer wears a flowery apron and no longer lives near the top of a tower block looking down on the rest of the world.

The nurse looks up: 'Do you want to feed her?'

Before I can answer, the bowl is in my hand and she walks out. Leaving us alone. It's the first time I can remember ever being alone with my grandma.

Is this it? Is this what happens? When did you get in this state? Are you really her?

'Come on, Grandma, have a bit.'

She refuses. Again and again.

'Stubborn as ever,' I say.

A flash in the eye. Was that recognition from Grandma? Whatever it was brings me back to being scared of her. I think she's still there, hiding, waiting to come out, still able to rule. I run to the door.

'Nurse, come back. You will have to feed her, she won't take it from me.'

With the nurse expertly feeding Grandma again, I think

to try talking to her again. No spark in her eye comes, no recognition; just weird noises escape from her mouth.

'I don't understand, Grandma. What's wrong? Do you know who I am? I am Hope.'

'She has senile dementia, love. Good days and bad days, it was a good day when she asked for you by name, but today is a bad day, so she won't understand you and she won't remember you, won't even know she has family. Last person that came to visit her was over a year ago. She was drunk so didn't stay long. Wanted money as I recall. Poor ol' thing.'

I am just staring. *How can things come to this? How can you end up so alone? What will happen to her in the future? What's happening to her? Poor old cow.*

The nurse interrupts my thoughts: 'Hope, your lift is here. Say goodbye now.'

I am unable to touch her hand, although I want to squeeze it. I've never touched my grandma, and that fills me with a sadness that overwhelms me. I realize that all three of this woman's children were taken into care, as were several of her grandchildren. She's been physically and emotionally alone throughout her life. I am not sure what to say, so I just say what I think I should:

'Goodbye, Grandma. Take care of yourself.'

19

A DIFFERENT FORM OF REBEL

Notes, taken by Hope, in 1993, from social services files:
Letter – my official solicitor to the Supreme Court: 20 June 1988
Re: Hope Daniels

— Writing re letter 7 April 1988 from Supreme Court – that
letter indicated that a fostering social worker was allocated
to Hope Daniel's case.

— Asks for update as progress has not yet been made to find
foster parents for Hope, who has recently moved to Beaufort.

Closed file, 1988
*I'll show them. People comin' in and out of my life all the time.
No one fuckin' stays. No one fucking wants me.*

The pillow is soaked with my tears and snot, in response
to the solicitor's letter I asked for. All I get is the realization
that Hackney Social Services has closed my fostering file
and a pain that feels like it has cut me down the middle, to
my core. I've kicked and punched the end of my bed, but I
don't feel any pain in my hands, just inside, screaming to

get out. Pain is pouring out of me at the injustice of it all in the form of salty tears and ending up on my bedclothes.

Why oh why? Why me, why do they always make promises then take them away? There were loads of letters in response to my picture.

Even Erica's mum applied, but she was turned down as she is a single mother. My fostering social worker and key worker spent ages going through all the letters, sifting out the weirdos from the normal ones. At the end, they told me about three families.

For a while, I bounced around, catching my smiling face in the mirror, stopping and play-acting the introduction to my new family. I have seen 'meet the parents' so many times before, happening to other kids, and now I thought it was my turn. I imagined my new life in their happy home, in a home where they had chosen me, in a home where I was wanted. One of the three families lived in a house right on the edge of a graveyard, so no thank you to that. My key worker visited them. One family, an aerobics teacher and a fireman, were perfect. When I was told they wanted to meet me, feelings I'd never had before, of fear and happiness all mixed together, went rushing around my brain so I felt faint. Then nothing. I asked and asked:

'When will I meet them?'

Eventually they said my fostering social worker had gone on maternity leave and the key worker was waiting for them to find another one. This morning the key worker came to Beaufort and told me that as Social Services didn't find another fostering social worker for me, I'm too late for the aerobics instructor and the fireman as they have chosen another little girl. I am too stunned to respond, thoughts zoom around my head, taunting me.

No wonder Betty told me there was no one suitable that replied to the advert. Why did the fostering social worker tell me there was a fireman and an aerobics lady? Why? Why? Why did they build up my hope and dreams. Why couldn't they find me a new fostering social worker? Or did the foster parents read my file and not want me? No one wants me. I'm a horrid person.

As there is no one else on my fostering file, Hackney Social Services have closed my fostering case. So now I lie face down on my bed, having already made use of my cutting kit, and I sob.

Just like that. They turned down Erica's mum, the aerobics instructor and the fireman didn't want me. Social services are stopping me having a family. I hate them. I hate them.

Notes, taken by Hope, in 1993, from social services files:
— 12 July 1988: absconded yet again. Went missing from Beaufort on the afternoon of 10th July – not yet returned.
— Returned on 12 July. Phoned from London asking if weekend to visit brothers was going to be stopped. When we told her it was not, she returned.
— Had a discussion with Hope about the future & responsibility to herself.
— Reminded her about her educational possibilities, being a bright girl – if she applied herself then she could be a lawyer, doctor or other such profession.
— It's up to her to break the cycle, and an education here equals stability. Hope visited her brothers, as planned, and returned on schedule.

Visiting home, 23 December 1988

The broken old door is off the latch as it always has been. I push it open, looking back at my friend who is waiting across the street for me. I did want her to come with me, but now I don't.

'Hi, Dad, where's Mum?'

'Upstairs.'

What about 'Hello, Hope, How are you?' Is that too much to ask? Mum is upstairs . . .

'What's that noise, Dad?'

'Oh you know . . .'

Yes I know . . . Die, you dirty old man. Die, you dirty old man.

There is a whisky bottle on the table, in the same place there has always been a whisky bottle, and my dad is sitting beside it in the same place he always sits. My dad looks older, more grey. The stairs creak, as the man who has been visiting my mother departs. She announces her arrival, and my visit with:

'Where the fuck have you been, you little bitch, and why the fuck haven't you come to see us sooner?'

'I don't know, Mum, just been busy, you know. I did come last week, with the social worker, like we arranged, but you weren't here.'

'Yeah, like we told yer fuckin' social worker, we didn't know you were coming, no one told us. It was a Monday, you know we always go out on Monday. But it's been months, Hope, your poor ol' dad and me, struggling to get by while you are swanning around in your new jeans and your new home. You're as ugly as ever though, you need to wear a bit of make-up. How old are you now, thirteen?'

'I was fourteen last birthday, Mum, not that you remembered.'

'What the fuck did you say? How the fuck are we supposed to remember, when you gave us all these problems? Selfish cow, grassin' us up, leaving us here to fend for ourselves, doing what we have to do to get by . . .'

Why did you have to have a man here. Why couldn't you keep it special for us?

'I'm sorry, Mum.'

'So you fuckin' should be, now pour your dad and me a drink. You know where it is, nothing's changed. Do you want one?'

Standing in the hallway some fifteen minutes later, automatically avoiding the floorboard that creaks, I reach into my pocket searching for anything sharp. The anger building up inside me, I want to release it, but this time cutting my legs or arms in secret isn't enough. *I hate her so much. She doesn't care. She doesn't want you.*

The only thing I find is a key ring, one of my collection, and without hesitation I accept the urge to gouge my face and release the pain that bubbles to the surface from deep within.

I am in front of the mirror, yet I close my eyes. I just want to feel the pain inside being released as I scratch, released so I can cope with this mess that is my life again. I want to leave the pain and guilt here, to leave her and never see her again. From the top of my cheekbone to my chin, again and again I scratch until I feel a little better, and I open my eyes in the mirror. Standing looking back at me, is a sad child, who should have been able to cry, but has found another way to cope. Instead of tears, there are tracks of blood running down my face.

Without saying goodbye, or looking round the house, I open the door, take it off the latch and close it behind me.

'Fuckin' hell, what happened to you?'

'My mum.'

Notes taken by Hope, in 1993, from social services files:
Extract from Beaufort miscellaneous report, 20 August 1989.

Hope has, despite the challenges she faces, settled into her work. Asked for extra lessons to catch up, and has not absconded for a month. She is in receipt of rewards points – is doing well and earning treats and rewards.

20

DESTABALISING ACTION

Notes, taken by Hope, in 1993, from social services files:
Beaufort school report, March 1990

— Hope has managed to maintain a positive approach to her education despite uncertainties this term – being unsettling.
— Even though there have been personal problems outside the classroom she made excellent progress.
— Taking a wide range of exams – should obtain good results.
— Hope has the ability to continue her education to a higher level.

Celebrating, 1990

'Fuckin' 'ell!'

'Language, Hope!'

We are in McDonald's, celebrating. It's the first time I've come here and not been told I'm moving or getting locked up – or been told by Mum and Dad to lie for them. I'm here for the reason a child should be here, to celebrate a good school report. I know I've worked really hard, but I still think they are lying.

'Sorry, I just can't believe my school report, they are shittin' me. It's so fuckin', sorry, it's soooo good.'

'Careful you don't get tomato sauce on it. And it's only good because you've worked so hard. I hear you've taken extra lessons and applied all that energy into study.'

'Is nothing secret?' But I'm smiling, so she knows I'm joking. 'Really, do you really think I can go on to a higher level?'

'Of course. You are very bright, and have caught up quickly.'

'Well, I worked hard, I did all the extra lessons.'

'What would you like to be, Hope?'

I stare for a long time at the insides of my burger bun. The sauce is dripping off it. *Should I reveal what I want to be? It's a stupid thought, isn't it?*

I take a deep breath.

'I'd like to be a lawyer.'

'Really? That is fantastic. Why?'

'Well, because I never get to go into court, or into the case meetings, and I want to be able to do the right thing for other people that can't get into the room.'

'Excellent, you've really thought this through. Let me take that back and see what we can do. You are very bright, resourceful and a hard worker, when you apply yourself, Hope, so I can see this happening.'

Cheekily, I add: 'Can I come into the meeting where they decide whether or not I can become a lawyer?'

'You know you can't, Hope.'

We both smile at each other. The possibilities stretch out

of my mind, through the door of McDonald's and into the High Court, where one day I will stand, as a lawyer, making my own case.

'Hope, Hope, where are you, Hope?'

I come rushing out of the living-room.

'What is it, what's happened?'

'Your letter did it, Hope, it swung them. The council has agreed to fund you as long as you stay in education. They will fund you right the way until you become a lawyer.'

The whole place erupts in cheers and shouts of 'Well done!', lots of them, so does that make them 'Well dones'? I make a note that I will need to check the dictionary. My teacher told me to do that whenever I want to know what something means or how to spell it.

I'm the first person I know that this has happened to. I smile to myself, as I know it's 'cos I had an input into the meeting. I wrote them a letter. My chest fills full of air, puffed out like a frigate bird I saw on the telly. My eyes well with happy tears, and someone hands me a tissue.

The noise of the home celebrating on my behalf allows me to step back as if I'm watching it all. It's like I am outside looking in. Suddenly the cheers take me back into a whisky-filled room where my family are celebrating the receipt of unpaid benefits.

Oh, how things could have been different if we had just had that money at the right time. Oh, Daddy, I wish you could see me now. I wish you could see this and be proud of me.

Meetings, 1990

'Hope, will you come downstairs, please? We have something to discuss with you.'

Stuff like this always sends me into a panic. *What have I done wrong? I've been really fuckin' good this last eighteen months. Has someone set me up? Has someone grassed me up for something I didn't do? Crap, crap. What do they want?*

'Only one way to find out, that's to go.' Even though I say this out loud there is no one in the room, except my Duran Duran posters. Of course, I am going to marry Simon Le Bon. The fact he's been married for five years now gives me a chance. Marriage doesn't last that long.

'Wish me luck,' I say to the poster, and I know Simon does.

Walking into the office, with a smile on my face that could charm anyone, I see an empty chair waiting for me. The principal as well as my counsellor are waiting in silence for me, sitting straight-backed in office chairs that won't let you do anything else but sit up straight.

Crap, what have I done? Best shut up, Hope, and hear them out.

The principal speaks first. This must be serious.

'Hope, you have done really well in the last eighteen months, and we are really proud of all you have achieved and your ambitions to be a lawyer. We have really enjoyed watching you develop here at Beaufort, but . . .'

She lowers her eyes, slowly, delaying the words after the 'but', as if that will make a difference. I watch and say nothing, sitting stock still as my mind races round the track.

Here we go, the let-down is coming. They don't want me,

that's what it is. They are just like everyone else. They don't want me. They've just been pretending.

'The fact that you have taken on extra lessons, are working at the weekends in the bakery, have not run away and to our knowledge stayed sober . . .'

She looks up and smiles.

Get on with it. If you are chucking me out, if you have listened to someone's lies about me, get on with it.

'Well we feel . . .'

A look passes between the two women, a silent 'We are doing the right thing here?' or was it 'Are we doing the right thing here?' My counsellor nods just so you can see it, but no more. I don't think I am meant to see the nod.

Well, you're not doing the right thing. I want to scream. I know what is coming.

'Well, we feel that you are ready to move to another unit, still within Beaufort, but another unit, more suited to you.'

I hesitate before replying.

'Why do I have to move? What have I done wrong?'

'You've done nothing wrong, Hope, it will just be better for you.'

'Will I have the same staff, the same counsellor, the same room?'

'No, Hope, these things will all be different, but you will settle in soon.'

'When?'

'In a week or so, when you've got used to the idea.'

New rules. Change, change, change. Why can't they just leave me now I'm settled? I don't want to move. I want to stay. People care for me here, although you don't want me.

Already crying, I stand. For the first time in my life I say nothing, I just turn, open the door and walk away to my bedroom, my back to them as the tears roll down my face.

A knock on my door brings one of the female staff sneaking in. Why does she have to tiptoe? She strokes my hair and hands me the number for an organization she says can help me: Voice for the Child in Care.

'Call them for advice,' is all she says, leaving the paper on the bedside table then stealing away again, leaving me with my red eyes, runny nose and a dark feeling of rejection, fear and devastation that yet again, even though I try to please everyone, no one wants me. A snot bubble escapes, 'cos on top of all that, I never seem to have enough tissues.

My feet won't stop tapping the floor. My knee is going up and down, juddering like a sewing machine needle. I think I'm trying to get rid of lots of excess energy that has built up since I called Voice for the Child in Care. Waiting for this meeting has been making me nervous and excited at the same time. I worry they too will let me down, so I've tried to make a good impression.

I am wearing my best jeans and my nicest top. My hair is pulled back from my face into a high ponytail, so I look smart, and now I wait. I only have thirty minutes' lunch break from the bakery, so I hope she isn't late. An advocate, they called her.

Thirty minutes later, I leave the meeting with a plan. The letter I have to write to the board of Beaufort is already formulating in my brain. The resolve of refusing to move, refusing to pack up my room, and if they still move me, refusing to unpack my room, gives me a new feeling. One of control over my own life, and I like this feeling. I am taking responsibility for myself, and tonight instead of going out, I shall write my letter to the board and the management explaining my case. The reasons I shouldn't move and how this move, according to the notes in my bag and advice from the advocate, is 'disruptive', and 'detrimental' to my well-being. Especially with my GCSEs coming up. These are the words we agreed upon in the meeting. As I walk home, I realize this is the first meeting I have been to with a professional where I'm making decisions about myself.

Voice for the Child in Care says to wait a few more days for a response to my letter. I handed it in personally to everyone on the management team, and put it in the pigeonholes for the board. This is where their letters go, so I know everyone got one. No one has replied. I want them to reply. To tell me it's OK to stay in my lovely room. I think I made a very good case for staying, and looked a lot of words up in the dictionary, so I have learnt a lot in the process too.

The head of my unit is waiting for me at the front door. She looks like she has no expression on her face at all. I don't know how people can do that. No expression. With me it's written all over my face, all the time. I like that.

'Hope, while you were at work today you've been moved to the new unit. Here, I will take you to your new room.'

I can tell from her change in expression that my face says it all. Dejected, unloved, not listened to. Worthless.

That's what I am, worthless. My opinion doesn't count for nothin'.

My new room is dark and unfriendly, and all my boxes are piled high.

'I will never unpack them boxes, you know.'

Boxes, 1990

I lie in bed and am scared that for the last few months I've lost the ability to feel, to care. I don't think it will come back to me. No one cares about me, so why should I care about them? No one cares about me, not even me. Grandma died last week, and they didn't tell me about the funeral. Had she been better, I know she would have come and got me, and taken me home to her flat, looked after me. She was the only one who ever wanted me, or so I like to think. But she's dead now, and in her box in the ground, so I will never know how much she cared. Although, I think that maybe she was cremated, and not put in a box all alone with just the worms for company.

My cardboard boxes with all my things gathering dust inside are still piled high along the left-hand side of my room. They are stacked there, reminding me that no one cares what I think, and I don't care what they decide for me now, 'cos I make my own choices. I know now that, whatever I do, however I try to please people, to make them like me, I don't please people and they will do what they want anyway. All I can feel is anger and the headache I have from last night's drink and experimentation with drugs.

Shit, what was that shit I tried? I can't remember a fuckin' thing. Ha! Ha! I got a black cab home, though, and they had to pay! Just like my mum.

I feel a little duller inside at that thought. I look around. Apart from the packed boxes, in which Simon Le Bon and the rest of the band still live, the only visible thing in my room is the stuff I nicked, that I plan to sell for booze. I don't have any money now as I stopped working at the bakery after they moved me into this room. *No one loves me, and no one wants me, so why should I care?* These words embrace me like an old friend who welcomes me back to the fold. To where I should be, to the expected life of a child who's been in care, one who rebels by taking control of their own life and loses control; by being the best at meeting expectations. They don't expect us to achieve, so why should I try? The only people who ever cared are moved away, or I am moved away from them, like Erica and her mum. You can't rely on no one but yourself, and you can't trust adults as they get you settled then move you on.

I can get by as I always did, begging, stealing and charming folk. It's always worked before. Who needs an education, who wants to become a lawyer anyway? It was a pathetic idea, stupid thought.

Shit it's scary, I wouldn't fit into that lifestyle of being a lawyer. I am the most horrible girl, and I've been rejected for the last time. I can't go to college and be a lawyer, I wouldn't fit in, and I couldn't do it anyway.

Every time I try to do something outside of what's expected of a child in care, it all just gets chucked in the air again, all changes. They move you constantly, no one wants you around, 'cos they don't think you're worth anything. No one wants me, and you can't drag yourself back from that.

What I'm good at is surviving, and caring for someone else. Then it comes to me, the life I want to lead, not a lawyer, but I want to be a mum, a good mum. A child would give me someone to love, someone who can't reject me. Someone who I love and who loves me. Someone I wouldn't do drugs for. A family, my family, a happy family. I can hold a family together, with a child who I love. That I can do. With my brothers, I've been doing it all my life.

21

THE FILES

Back again, 1996

I look at my baby girl, cute as a button at three years old. Despite her being planned to get me out of the home, I've no regrets.

She is the definition of love.

I'm back in the same room I was in when I was eighteen. The files are waiting for me once again. My obsession with them has not disappeared. It feels like there is an invisible cord that draws me to them, my life in brown folders. There they are sitting on the Formica table, like they haven't moved in the three years since I last saw them.

They are still there, there are still thirteen of them, but this time the newest file is fatter than it was. I know what is in there though: my falling pregnant, my marriage, my daughter. Achieving nine GCSEs then turning my back on an education. Following the expected path of a child leaving care. I sigh.

'Do you want some pencils and paper? Can you please

do Mummy a drawing, while Mummy looks at these things over here?'

She accepts a pencil and paper, sits down on the floor on the blanket I've brought with me for her. She looks up and smiles. My heart melts.

There is nothing like the smile of a child to make you happy.

I turn back to the table, pulling out my notebook from my bag and the chair that is also waiting for me. Another sigh escapes. Unlike three years ago, this time I am prepared. My right hand reaches forward and pulls out one of the old and worn files. It sits in front of me. I take another deep breath as I open the brown protective cover. I look at the first page and a sense of calm takes over. I am ready to know what happened behind the scenes, in the social workers' meetings and to my parents and brothers. I shift my bum in my chair and settle in to read the other side of the story.

Hours later, I lean back in the chair. My body is stiff from hunching over, my eyes tired from reading so much. I stretch my arms out in front of me, then raise them above my head, feeling the tension in my muscles release. I rub my forehead, wishing that the tension there would disappear as easily.

Enough.

I look round the room. There are used tissues all around my chair, each one having captured my tears before being discarded. My daughter is asleep in her pushchair. Her falling asleep gifted me the precious time to read the professional adult view of my life as a child, one page at a time. Now, emotionally, I am drained.

She's still asleep, so just one more file.

I reach out – this one is from three years after we left home. I take notes:

Extract from social worker's report, 13 February 1986

— Is everyone in agreement that rehabilitation is no longer appropriate? The plan now is to place the children with a permanent substitute family.

— It's agreed.

— Birth parents are unable to cope with care of the children, have continuing problems of abuse and related social and financial difficulties. These have not really abated since the children have been in care ...

— Goal of placement is long-term fostering, not adoption. Children are wards of court so permission to place would have to be sought from the wardship court, but no problems are anticipated.

— Under the new 'system' the family would have to be found before the court can be consulted.

— The committee stresses that the goal is to place the family together.

I feel like a truck has been driven through me.

What happened? Why were we not placed? Why were we not told of this decision? Why did we not get fostered? This said we should have been fostered. I was always told it was not an option.

My head is spinning. The files are all over the floor. I don't remember pushing them there, my hands are holding my head, and my daughter is crying. I pick her up.

'It's all right, baby, it's OK. Mummy just got a fright.'

Out of my bag, I pull her beaker of juice. I feed my daughter, calm her.

* * *

At home, my baby is settled, asleep, calm. She is the most precious and beautiful thing to me. *My mother missed so much, of us, of you. Mummy, Daddy, what did you do?*

A tear falls from my face onto the pillow beside you. I make a silent promise to myself, to you.

Whatever happened, happens, to me in my life, you, my sweet child, will be protected from it all. I will make sure you are safe, secure and happy.

I go downstairs to sit alone with my thoughts. The words from the files reappear at the front of my brain, and swirl around the room, tormenting me.

It should have been different.

I stare with disgust at the drink in my glass, yet still I lift the vodka to my lips. There is another voice, deep inside me. I almost acknowledge this inner voice telling me that, just as the files have done over the years, vodka is now calling me.

Who doesn't have a drink after a long, emotionally challenging day? Nothing wrong with it.

As the cool alcoholic medicine slips down my throat, I start to forget all the things I read in the files today. I have obsessed about knowing what was in them: now I know. This new information has transferred from the page into my brain. By doing so it has created a volcano of emotions I don't understand. I feel weak. My head hurts. The world as I know it has been turned upside down. Nothing will ever look the same.

Why couldn't I have been happy knowing what I knew?

There is a voice in my head.

I wish I had never started.

POSTSCRIPT

A Letter to my Daddy, March 2010

Dear Daddy,

Remember, I always called you that, even when I was an adult! Oh how I would love to show you how well I have done with Lucy and Jake. You would be so happy to be a great grand-dad, but I truly believe that you do know, and that you can see me from above.

I felt compelled to start writing this letter this morning, at the age of thirty-five, after remembering our lovely days, of which I am so grateful there were some. Especially when we would spend our days together in Hamilton Street, on my day visits from Chesterfields. Remember our bingo sessions! You were always so peeved that you didn't win, that I willed you a lucky break, alas, for it did not come.

Daddy, I don't want to feel angry with you, but now that I have successfully found recovery, I wonder, often, why you couldn't do that for us. Of course, I know, that if you don't enter recovery for yourself, it doesn't work, but that's my programme talking. Emotions aren't so straightforward, are they? Mum told me after you passed away, that you never really got over the guilt of losing us, and remembering this finally brought me compassion and empathy for your addiction, but not some of your actions. I've tried to lose the bitterness and anger, whilst never losing the irony of finding myself in the grips of the very same addiction.

This doesn't stop the questions streaming through my head, triggered by a memory sparked off by a reminder of the good and bad times. This morning, our favourite TV programme we would watch together – Big Daddy wrestling Giant Haystacks, remember?! – came to my mind. Then followed the big question which used to plague me as a teenager. How could you sell your wife to other men? How could you sit downstairs, knowing that another man was using your wife for their own needs? How could you allow men into the bedroom I shared with you, or did you not know that Mum did those things in the same room as I slept? The danger you both put me in, makes me shudder.

One of the many things you didn't know about me, Dad, was that when I was eighteen I started reading my Social Services files, whilst I was pregnant with your granddaughter. Reading the files, up to where I just had to stop, crucified me, and still I would visit you and Mum, knowing what I had read in those files. Your addiction had taken you both to the depths of degradation, and yet you carried on. I just couldn't understand. The files blasted my fairy-tale story that I had built up in my mind all the way throughout my childhood: that if only you had both been given the help and support to deal with your addiction, you would have given up drinking, accepted you were alcohol-dependent, and been able to stop drinking and keep us. How simplistic a child's view is eh!

Your grandson has lots of your lovely, kind, generous ways, always buying me a present when he should be buying something for himself. Remember you used to do that for Mum? It must be in the genes, a thought I don't think lightly, as the dread I carry with me is that the genetic link of addiction may also lie dormant in my children, waiting to bite us back. I believe though, Dad, that I have now broken the nurture part of the risk, but that the nature may still remain.

When I was in my twenties, you and Mum didn't know that, once again, I sought the information of my childhood through the Social Services files. All thirteen volumes of them. Six months of weekly visits, to Hackney, knowing you were only a 10-minute bus ride away, the number 73, the same bus which always brings back disgusting flashbacks, of why Mum boarded that bus on a weekly basis. You know what I'm talking about.

I would sit there at home, on my rare visits to your home, pouring your drinks for you, after the alcohol had ruined your physical health to such a point that you were stuck in a wheelchair, virtually blind, leaving you unable to continue your addiction without a colluder, a role I took up out of pity.

You didn't know that I had read your terribly sad childhood papers. I learnt how you had been abandoned on the steps of a Barnado's home at the approximate age of eighteen months, by your dad, who couldn't cope after losing your mum to childbirth, your birth. And then when your dad remarried, he came back to claim you at fourteen, then sold your brown suit, which Barnardo's issued to all boys who left the home, and took you straight back to the Barnardo's doors again. I can't imagine how that felt. I often wonder whether you were excited, nervous and angry or just devoid of any feeling. My heart breaks when I think of the terrible way your dad used you, such horrible behaviour.

But it's not surprising, as according to the records, he too was alcohol-dependent; you see, Dad, the definition of insanity, repeating the same behaviour, and expecting a different result, doesn't make sense, does it?

You see, Dad, I know, that however bad your cravings got for the devil drink, you never ever would have done that to us.

When I took the scary first steps into recovery, and started the long healing process, I learnt about forgiveness. I knew that I didn't want the past to play a part in my family's new future, but I had no idea how I could forgive you for the loss and the pain. I thank God that my mind was open to the practice of forgiveness, and for the freedom it has given me.

I refuse to allow myself to spend my life eaten up by resentment, and this is why, through recovery, I found a way to truly forgive you. You see, if you break down 'resentment', it reads, 're-sent'. Re-sent from the past. My children and grandchildren and I refund that choice back to you!

Dad, I believe you too are now free from the pain of addiction, and wish you love, care and choice – the choice to avoid my mum at all costs if she meets you up there!!!

Much love
Hope
X

                                  (As originally written by Hope)

ACKNOWLEDGEMENTS AND A CLOSING NOTE

From Hope
Without my children's and husband's support, my story would never have got into print, and for that, I'm forever thankful. I love you all.

I want to make a special mention of my social workers, and in particular 'S', who has never stopped sharing her love, kindness and compassion, and whom I will love forever.

Lastly, I wish to thank Morag. Morag, you are one special woman: thank you so much.

From both Hope and Morag
It is of course necessary to protect the identities of many of the people that Hope came into contact with while growing up, and to do this, we have, with the exception of names and places in the public domain, protected identities by changing names, ages, street names and altering

some background details. We thank all of you who supported Hope as she grew up.

Our heartfelt thanks to all of those who have helped in the development of this book especially to those who are working to bring *Hackney Child* to a wider audience. Specifically to our agent Rebecca Winfield, for your enthusiasm, focus, and being the agent who brought the team at Simon & Schuster to us, thank you. Shirley Coomber, Graphic Designer and all at Town & Country Housing Group who kindly donated resources. Ruth Neville, Social Worker, Huddersfield University, who totally believes in Hope. Sir Martin Narey, Government Adviser, you are a seriously cool geezer! Lastly, but by no means least, all at Simon & Schuster who have recently worked on *Hackney Child*, thank you very much. Specifically, to our editor Kerri Sharp for supporting us – your big picture view, alongside gentle and detailed edits have brought this book to the next level, thank you for this and for your instantaneous, and continued, belief in *Hackney Child*.

We are so very happy and excited about these collective talents, thank you one and all. What a team we have, we are blessed.

From Morag to Hope

There are the birthdays we all remember, and then there are the birthdays you had. There are the crap days we all have, and then there are the crap days you had. Writing this book with you has opened a window onto a world that was hidden to me; a world that should have been better for you. Many times we have cried, and laughed, both together and in our own private space. What I find so powerful is that it is all true, and that you survived; you came through what is now thankfully in the past, to create a happy family of your own. Despite all that has happened, you smile, laugh and show the rest of us how life should be lived. I wish all the future birthdays, and all present and future days, are as you want, deserve and wish them to be. We have travelled a journey together. I do not have enough words to express all the admiration, respect and friendship that I have for you. Thank you for choosing me to be your voice, and thank you for being you.

If you would like to contact Hope, please do so via the following:

https://www.facebook.com/hackneychild

hackneychild@gmail.com